151
Quick Ideas

to
Recognize and
Reward Employees

By Ken Lloyd, Ph.D.

CAREER
PRESS
Franklin Lakes, NJ

151 QUICK IDEAS TO RECOGNIZE AND REWARD EMPLOYEES
EDITED BY KRISTEN PARKES
TYPESET BY KATE HENCHES
Cover design by Ark Stein/Visual Group
Printed in the U.S.A. by Book-mart Press

To order this title, please call toll-free 1-800-CAREER-1 (NJ and Canada: 201-848-0310) to order using VISA or MasterCard, or for further information on books from Career Press.

The Career Press, Inc., 3 Tice Road, PO Box 687,
Franklin Lakes, NJ 07417
www.careerpress.com

Library of Congress Cataloging-in-Publication Data
Lloyd, Kenneth L.
    151 quick ideas to recognize and reward employees / by Ken Lloyd.
        p. cm.
    Includes index.
    ISBN-13: 978-156414-945-9
    ISBN-10: 1-56414-945-5
        1. Incentives in industry. 2. Incentive awards. I. Title. II. One hundred fifty-one quick ideas to recognize and reward employees.

HF5549.5.I5L538 2007

                                658.3'142--dc22

Contents

How to Use This Book

This book is filled with proven recognition and reward strategies to help you build your employees' self-esteem, job satisfaction, and productivity.

Just as you would not go to a restaurant and order every item on the menu at one sitting, you should not try to apply all of these ideas at once. The best approach is to read through the book and take the following steps:

- ◆ Circle the ideas you like best.
- ◆ Highlight the ones you can start now.
- ◆ Set longer-term dates to implement your other favorites.
- ◆ Come back to the book every 90 days to select additional ideas.

Give your employees copies of this book and meet with them to discuss the ideas they like best, and set some dates to implement those that are feasible as well. If you want to use a particular idea, but it does not perfectly fit your company, do a little brainstorming with your team and you will most likely come up with a perfect solution.

It is important to remember that all of the ideas in this book have been successfully applied in businesses large and small throughout the world. And there is every reason to believe they will have an equally successful impact in your company!

Use Your Words

One of the most compelling, powerful, and effective ways to reward and recognize your employees is also the cheapest. All you have to do is open your mouth and give your employees the thanks and appreciation they deserve for a job well done. When employees hear you say, "Great job!" they feel better about themselves, their work, and the company itself, and this motivates them toward even higher levels of performance so they'll receive more of this feedback in the future.

The best time to provide this type of credit and recognition is as close to the employee's excellent behavior as possible. If you can give this feedback in front of other employees, the impact is even greater. Those other employees will start to think about ways they can improve their performance so they can be on the receiving end of praise from you.

Assignment

If you only use the words "Great job!" after your employees perform well, the words can lose their impact. Make a list of at least 20 of the most energizing and enthusiastic words you can use, such as "Terrific work!" "Outstanding performance!" "Amazing outcome!" and "Dazzling results!"

Epilogue
Employees continue to hear your positive words long after you have spoken them.

2

Set the Tone

Rewards and recognition do not exist in a vacuum, and their impact hinges on the workplace context and culture. If the environment is harsh or cold, all of your efforts to reward and recognize employees will fall short. For example, if a manager typically treats employees with indifference, any positive feedback or rewards he or she provides will be received with skepticism at best. However, the same feedback or rewards from a more supportive manager will be well received. As a result, if you want rewards and recognition to work, it is essential to set a tone that is positive, friendly, fair, and premised on respect and trust.

Assignment

Look over the listing of employees in your department and related areas and put a "+" next to those you regularly greet, a "0" next to those you occasionally greet, and a "−" next to those you rarely or never greet. Now set a timetable to make all of them a "+."

One easy way to help set this tone is to avoid the common managerial practice of looking through employees rather than talking to them. By saying "hello" to your employees around the office, perhaps asking how things are going, and then listening, your employees are going to feel appreciated, important, and respected, and these are great rewards.

Epilogue

Employees who rarely hear "hello" from their manager find it much easier to say "good bye."

3

Drop on By

A powerful source of recognition for your employees is the level of interest that you focus on them and their work. If you are inaccessible or basically invisible, your employees can easily sense they are not particularly valuable to you or the company. When you manage by wandering around, one advantage is that you can use all of your senses to get a better idea of how a department is operating.

On a more subtle level, by spending time in your employees' work areas, you are rewarding your employees. You are essentially telling them that although you have a great deal of important work that needs your attention, your team is even more important. Your visits are not based upon resolving a specific problem, and they are free of any agenda other than a desire to meet with the employees, see how things are going, ask a few questions, and answer even more.

> ### *Assignment*
>
> Write down the number of times per day that you visit your team without any specific agenda or scheduled meeting. If you are averaging less than one visit per day, commit right now to move that average to more than one visit per day.

You are not bearing gifts nor are you doling out cash. You are providing ongoing psychological rewards that build the employees' sense of self-worth and competence.

Epilogue
Your presence is often the best present you can give your employees.

4

Let's Get Formal

Regardless of the informal thanks, credit, and recognition you give to your employees, a great source of meaningful rewards for them comes from receiving formal feedback on their performance at least once a year.

Many managers tend to delay these sit-down meetings or forget about them altogether, typically mouthing the mantra, "I don't have time." This type of thinking destroys a valuable recognition opportunity.

Assignment

First, set a date to meet with each of your employees to review their performance. Second, set a time a few days ahead of this meeting to get prepared and look over your employees' performance and notes you may have made during informal meetings with them during this period.

It is highly rewarding for an employee to have a clear idea of how he or she is doing and where improvement may be needed. When an employee is not given this feedback, it is akin to shooting arrows at a target, but not seeing where they are hitting.

The most obvious messages in formal review sessions deal with the employees' performance, but the deeper message is that you have a genuine interest in the employees and their careers, and this is one of the greatest rewards you can provide.

Epilogue

If you want to have a meeting of the minds with your employees, no one will mind if you start with a meeting.

The Riches of Enrichment

Employees sense high levels of recognition and reward when management enriches their jobs. Some managers operate under the misconception that enrichment means giving employees more work, typically more of the same work. This is merely expanding their jobs horizontally. In this scenario, rather than feeling rewarded, employees feel used.

Real enrichment expands the employees' jobs vertically by providing them with more autonomy, control, and decision-making responsibilities. They are given increased opportunities to think and grow, and, in many respects, they are able to act as managers of their own jobs. When jobs are truly enriched, employee performance improves in many different ways, especially in terms of the quality of their work.

> ### Assignment
>
> At some point, hopefully in the near future, all of your employees will be ready for job enrichment. To help prepare for this, look over each employee's job and list at least five specific ways to enrich it.

Job enrichment is not simply handed to all employees, but rather is earned by those whose performance is consistently strong. It is a reward for excellence, and employees in enriched positions tend to experience increased feelings of confidence, achievement, and personal competence.

Epilogue
When jobs are enriched, employees and their companies are enriched, too.

15

6

Nothing Like a Good Book

A great way to recognize and reward an employee is to give him or her a book. Obviously, you have millions of choices, but you can set some parameters by looking at the individual employee and the position he or she holds. Many of the best rewards are tailored to fit whoever is receiving them, and you can easily do this with a book.

For example, if you have an employee who has management potential, you can certainly give a book on management. However, you can just as easily give a novel that includes a character who displays outstanding managerial skills.

Assignment

Write down the names of each of your employees and then list two or three books that would be perfect for each of them. Order the books and have them ready for the next time one of these employees does something great.

If you want to make this reward more tailored or personalized, you can give a book that deals with the employee's hobbies or outside interests, or a well-reviewed book you believe your employee will enjoy.

Regardless of the book you select, you should personalize it by inscribing it. Use a good pen, write the employee a short praiseful note, and then sign and date it.

Epilogue

Giving a book without any inscription is like giving a trophy without any engraving.

The Art of Articles

Your employees like to know that you are thinking of them, and not just in a general sense, but also as individuals. One of the best ways to recognize their individuality is to send them an article that is particularly appropriate to their interests.

The article can deal with some work-related matters, or it can focus on your employee's general interests or hobbies. You can give the employee a hard copy of the article in person, or you can just as easily send it as an attachment. Either way, the message is clear: you regard this employee as a valued individual on your team.

In this way, you are actually providing two rewards. First, there is the psychological reward that comes from being remembered and recognized by one's manager. And, secondly, there is the tangible reward of the article itself.

When you give the article to the employee, be sure to attach a short note that includes the employee's name and a

> ## *Assignment*
>
> Make a list of your employees' objectives and interests, and then actively look for relevant articles. The objective is to send each employee at least one article every other month.

few positive words about how you thought this article ties right into this individual's goals, interests, or hobbies.

Epilogue

Articles that you provide to your employees help build unity—they are truly articles of confederation.

8

Turning the Corner

Every manager is going to have an employee who struggles. With a good deal of coaching, guidance, support, and perhaps a bit of luck, that employee may experience a turnaround.

When you have an employee who makes this kind of transition, you have a golden opportunity to provide some recognition. Recognition at this point is positive reinforcement that will encourage this employee to continue his or her successful behaviors.

This employee should be given an award indicating that he or she is the most improved player. Whether at a special staff

> ### *Assignment*
>
> Make a list of your employees who are struggling. Note the key areas where they need to improve and the specific steps they should take. Meet with them, gather their inputs, and have them sign off on a document where they commit to taking these steps.

meeting or as part of a larger recognition program, employees who make great improvement should be singled out in front of the group and praised for their totally improved performance. They could be given a special award, the TIP Award for Totally Improved Performance, exclusively for employees who have tipped the scales and are now performing at a TIP-TOP level. This award can be accompanied by any number of goodies that are listed in forthcoming chapters.

Epilogue

Performance improvement is contagious, and it can easily be spread by recognition and rewards.

9

Subscription Recognition

It is quite rewarding for your employees to see that you are genuinely interested in their growth, development, and success, and one way for them to literally grasp your commitment in these areas is to give them a subscription to a magazine or journal that relates to their job responsibilities and objectives.

The subscription should be in the employee's name because this clearly focuses the recognition on the named individual. This can be a source of additional recognition if the employee then forwards the magazine to others who may be interested in one or more of the articles.

> ### *Assignment*
>
> Review the responsibilities and objectives of each of your employees, and then match them up with possible magazines or journals, whether hard copy or online. Let your employees know the magazines or journals you are considering, and then ask if they have a preference.

The recognition from the subscription can be further compounded if you let the employee know you would be glad to set up a departmental brown-bag lunch if there is an article he or she would like to discuss. The offer to run this type of discussion is rewarding in and of itself, and actually leading such a session offers additional opportunities for recognition.

Epilogue

Giving a magazine subscription is tantamount to giving a timed-release capsule that regularly provides a healthy dose of recognition.

10

What's Right Is Write

One of the most old-fashioned ways of providing recognition is also one of the most effective. Although many people find the notion of picking up a pen and writing anything to anyone an archaic and time-consuming task, it is a great way to show another individual that you have made an extra effort to recognize his or her accomplishment.

This does not mean that you have to write an epic novel or spew some fancy and flowing prose. A short handwritten note that specifically mentions the individual's name followed by words of praise for his or her success is always well received and well remembered.

A particularly interesting point is that many people are less likely to throw out a handwritten note. They tend to file it away, and then look back at it every once in a while. This means that your written note continues to provide recognition and good feelings well after you have put the pen back in your drawer.

Assignment

Take out a pen and paper and try this technique by writing a brief note of recognition to yourself for a recent success. When you read it, you are guaranteed to feel good. And when your employee gets one, he or she will feel even better.

Epilogue

A handwritten note gives your employees a hand today and tomorrow.

11

E-mail for Excellence

Another highly effective way to spell out credit and recognition for an employee is to send an e-mail that waxes glowingly over his or her accomplishment. The first step in writing this is to use upbeat language in the subject line, such as "Excellent Work!" or "Congratulations!"

The next step is to put the employee's name before any of the text you write. The tendency with office e-mail is to simply write a message, and this is fine for most online business communication, but not for a note of recognition.

A similar point applies to the end of this laudatory message. Before you hit "Send," be sure to include your name. Even though most business e-mail ends with the last sentence of the message, that is not enough for a laudatory note. If you really want to personalize it and emphasize the significance of your employee's accomplishment, add your name, and not with your title or phone extension under it.

> ### *Assignment*
>
> Take a look at your employees right now. There is at least one whose performance merits recognition today, but you have been too busy to provide it. Send this employee an e-mail that praises his or her work. And don't be surprised if you receive an equally appreciative e-mail in response.

Epilogue
When you give thanks, you get thanks. And more.

12

Going Virtually Wide

You can easily compound the power of your laudatory e-mail messages by clicking "cc" and simultaneously sending copies to various significant others in your organization. Taking this extra step has several compelling advantages, the first of which is that it makes the employee feel extra proud, positive, and pumped because his or her accomplishment has been placed before so many important eyeballs.

On a broader basis, by going wide with your message, you have helped put a spotlight on your employee that can help generate additional opportunities for his or her growth and advancement within the company. In addition, when your employees perform well, it also means that you have helped set the stage for their success. In this way, you are sending a positive message about yourself to topside management as well.

The icing on this corporate cake arrives when a topside manager sends a congratulatory note back to

Assignment

To save time down the road, write out a list of senior corporate players who should receive copies of the praiseful e-mail notes that you send to your employees for their accomplishments. Now put an asterisk by each topsider who might need a friendly prompt to send their own congratulatory note as well.

the employee. This feeds the employee a second portion of recognition, and that is very tasty indeed.

> **Epilogue**
> *When you make others look, you look good.*

13

Go for the Green

If you had a chance to provide recognition to a rapidly growing number of employees on a matter of real importance to them, you would probably jump at the opportunity. That's exactly what managers worldwide are doing right now when it comes to implementing programs that are environmentally friendly.

Eco-friendly steps span a huge spectrum that can include putting out organic

Assignment

Make a list of 10 actions that you can take in order to make your workplace more environmentally friendly. Rank each item in your list in terms of importance and cost, and then set a schedule to implement each over the next 12 months.

fruit for the employees, providing health-oriented perks, using recycled materials, switching to solar power, and even redesigning a company's ventilation system to reduce toxins in the air.

Although interest in going green is more common among young employees, it is shared by growing ranks of employees of all ages. When managers implement these types of programs, employees literally and figuratively feel better about working for the company, and the idea of working for such a forward-thinking company is a source of pride and recognition when describing their work to others.

It is profoundly rewarding for employees to sense that management is proactively taking steps to deal with issues that are meaningful to them.

Epilogue
When you are friendly to the environment, it is friendly to you.

14

Cards Online

It is always best to provide recognition as close to an employee's successful performance as possible, and you can do so at the speed of light by sending an online card.

There are numerous sites that offer cards for any occasion, and with a little searching, you can find one that perfectly fits the person and the situation. The nice thing about this type of recognition is that you are connecting with several of the employee's senses at the same time. With an online card, an employee's sense of touch, sound,

---

Assignment

Because timing is of the essence, go to any search engine and enter the phrase "online cards." Visit several sites and copy the addresses of those with cards that have the best fit with your team. If you see any cards that are particularly appropriate for your employees, write the employees' names next to the address.

---

and sight are all involved, and this makes the recognition all the more memorable.

When employees receive an online card, they tend to smile and feel good for the moment and beyond. After all, if the card fits really well, they are not likely to delete it. Rather, they will save it and return to it several times, repeatedly experiencing those good feelings of recognition.

Epilogue

Online cards are on time, on track, on target, and live on and on and on.

15
Cards Offline

Another highly effective way to provide recognition to your employees is to go traditional and select an appropriate greeting card from a bricks-and-mortar store. Even in today's virtual world, employees still appreciate holding a clever and attractive card that is meant solely for them.

25

Assignment

To avoid having to look for that perfect card at the last minute, make a list of the stores you frequent that have gift card sections. Set aside five minutes each time you visit these stores to look through the card section. Over the next month, commit to buying at least one card for each of your employees.

The key strategy is to select a card that not only fits the occasion, but also fits your employee's personality. Once you have selected that perfect card, be sure to add a few words of thanks or congratulations in your own handwriting, and then sign the card. If you simply sign your name, you are letting the card do all the talking, and that lessens its impact.

Also, do not just plop the card in your employee's mail slot or on his or her desk. The recognition will really hit home if you hand the card to the employee and offer a few words of thanks and recognition when doing so.

Epilogue
A great card for a great performance can have a great impact.

16

Take a Break

For the employees who have worked extra hard and attained outstanding results, an excellent reward is an afternoon or a full day off with pay. This type of recognition instantly shows that you appreciate your employees' diligence and dedication, and you understand the sacrifices they have made to get the job done.

This reward is best given as a surprise, rather than stipulated as a possible outcome if certain goals are met. If you present the possibility of time off at the outset of the project, but the project falls short or other time-consuming projects develop just as this one is wrapping up, there can be problems.

Besides, surprising an employee with time off is far more fun, and that's a great addition to any workplace. When you give out this reward, be sure to do so in person if possible, or at least by telephone. The more you personalize it, the greater its impact.

Assignment

Look carefully at the performance of each of your employees and see if there are any whose performance could merit a half day or full day off. For those who are in that range, look at the calendar for anticipated completion dates and anticipated projects for them, and then circle the possible days on which this time off could be given.

Epilogue

When employees work extra hard and are rewarded with extra time off, they return with extra energy, focus, and dedication.

17

Now Hear This

If you put a slight wrinkle on the notion of time off from work, you come up with another terrific way to reward your employees, namely the opportunity to go off-site to hear a great speaker. This reward gives your employees a combination of time off, education, information, and entertainment.

You can select from a vast array of speakers that includes management gurus, government leaders, prized athletes, military heroes, hot chefs, glitzy tycoons, newsmakers and shakers, heralded authors, hyper motivators, stand-up comedians, movie stars, and more. It is best to pick

Assignment

Almost every day there are newspaper announcements about speakers coming to your area. Make a list of these speakers, their topics, and appearance dates, and then match this list with the names of your employees who deserve to attend and whose interests and availability point to a good fit. Book them to attend and meet with them individually to give them the news.

speakers who can pique your employees' interests, as this will compound the reward and the enjoyment.

There is something exciting about seeing famous speakers in person, and there can even be more excitement when later telling friends and significant others about the event. When your employees return to work, a good piece of that excitement will come back with them.

Epilogue

When employees go off-site to hear an amazing speaker, there is far more than meets the eye—or the ears.

18

A Touch of Class

When employees perform well, one of the most meaningful rewards you can give them is an opportunity to attend seminars, classes, educational programs, or even pursue a degree. Employees typically have strong motivations to learn, grow, and develop, and rewards that help meet these needs are truly energizing.

You can now choose from a tremendous menu

Assignment

Make a list of your employees who merit this reward. Hopefully, it will be your entire team. Go to any major search engine and start the hunt for the perfect educational programs. Match each employee with programs that best fit their individual needs, skills, and objectives. When the time is right, let the school bells ring.

of educational options both online and off, and there are courses available on just about every imaginable subject. And further, there is a vast array of providers that includes public and private universities and colleges, private training companies, governmental training programs, professional associations, industry conventions, and numerous companies interested in training people to use their products.

With all of these options, you are now in a position to tailor any training to your individual employees. For example, some may respond well to supervisory or managerial training, while others will be far more appreciative of specific technical training. The better the fit, the better the reward.

Epilogue

Employee growth and development are the keys to a company's growth and development.

19

The Rewards of Teaching

After you have rewarded an employee by sending him or her to a seminar, class, course, or other educational program, you can take the reward to higher levels by inviting this individual to conduct a mini-seminar for the other employees. This mini-session would focus on the highlights of whatever your employee learned.

When you allow an employee to run an entire training session, you are fulfilling some of his or her most important psychological needs, namely the needs for recognition, responsibility, achievement, and growth. This step also rewards your employee with firsthand experience in public speaking, planning and organization, and training.

An additional benefit is that your employee will have to learn the course content particularly well in order to teach it. And, on a broader basis, this approach will increase the likelihood that the best content from the original program will actually be applied on the job.

Assignment

If you have any employees who recently attended an educational program, invite them to put on a mini-seminar for the rest of the team. To help make this session or any future sessions a success, take care of the administrative details such as reserving the meeting room, setting it up for the discussion, having notepads and pens ready, and ordering some light snacks.

Epilogue
When employees teach what they have learned, everyone learns some important lessons.

20

Certified and Bona Fide Leaders

A strategic management development program exclusive to your company can be a great source of recognition for your employees. This type of program, which can be designed by an internal team of managers or by an outside firm, provides your supervisory and managerial employees with a complete management development program.

Future managers and supervisors tend to learn most of their leadership skills from their own managers, typically through day-to-day interactions. Think about what you would teach your employees if you were to do so in a classroom. Develop a list of managerial topics where your expertise is particularly strong, and then develop a lesson plan to teach your employees in each of these areas.

Such a program is more than a bunch of classes loosely strung together and given a catchy label. Rather, this program includes a formal curriculum, regular classes both online and off, homework, and exams. Employees feel rewarded and special when selected to attend. They enjoy having the opportunity to learn and grow, and their inclusion implies that management recognizes them, respects them, and has positive expectations for them.

Beyond these intangible rewards, these programs are literally capped off with a graduation ceremony for those who complete the full curriculum. Each graduate is rewarded with a framed personalized diploma designating that they are certified supervisors and managers for your company.

Epilogue

When companies plant seeds of knowledge, the employees blossom.

21

Good Points

One of the best ways to connect a personalized reward with excellent behavior is to reward employees with points when they perform well. The employees can then take their points and use them to pick out any rewards they would like from various online reward sites. The more points they accumulate, the better the goods and goodies available to them.

One advantage of this approach is that you can give your employees their points immediately after they perform well. This type of instant gratification helps lock-in their stellar behavior. In addition, they enjoy any positive comments you might provide when lavishing these points upon them.

Assignment

Go to one of the major search engines and enter the keywords "online," "employee," and "rewards." Click on some of the online providers, review their product offerings and terms, and then select one that looks like the best fit for your company and your team. The one you select should provide you with everything you need to start this program right now.

The positive feelings continue when your employees go online to pick out their rewards. There is something particularly exciting about earning this type of shopping spree. When they do pick out that special reward, it is a perfect fit, and that makes any reward more long-lasting.

> **Epilogue**
> When employees can earn valuable points for performance, they engage in less pointless behavior.

22

Take Care of Yourself

Everyone wins when employees strive to maintain excellent health, and now there are cutting-edge steps you can take to reward your employees for pursuing healthier lifestyles. Some of the positive outcomes include richer and fuller lives, improved performance and attendance on the job, and even reduced insurance premiums.

Assignment

Contact your HR department or your company's health-care provider and ask about incentives for your employees and for the company if you implement a wellness program. If your provider gives you little more than a strange look, then you should look for another provider.

The idea is to establish a wellness program and reward employees who participate in it. There can be any number of rewards, such as a reduction in co-payments for doctor visits or prescription drugs. You can also offer reduced deductibles, or even cash or other tangible prizes.

Wellness programs typically require an initial doctor visit to check your employees' blood pressure, cholesterol, weight, and the like. Once this is completed, the employees who follow the doctor's instructions to improve their health are given the rewards.

When employees engage in healthier lifestyles, they often look and feel better, which is a great reward in and of itself. And when other tangible rewards are placed on top of this, it is not uncommon to find many employees hopping onto the healthier bandwagon.

Epilogue

Rewarding employees for a healthy lifestyle is a gift they will always carry.

23

Primo Parking

For employees who drive or carpool to work, the reward of a great parking space literally and figuratively has its place in an overall recognition program. A spot that is near the entrance is always appreciated, especially in outdoor lots during the hot, humid, or hazy months of the summer and the cold and icy months of winter.

Assignment

Take a look at your company's parking situation and select one spot that can be used for this reward program. Try to base this reward on performance that actually relates to driving to work, such as attendance, safety, or tardiness. The final step is to announce the program and conduct a drawing for all qualified employees.

There are some additional steps that can make this reward particularly appealing, such as giving the parking space a special designation. This can include a sign that prominently announces that it is reserved for company superstars, or special colored lines that distinguish this space from all others.

You can tack another reward onto this by posting online photos of the super employees as they proudly stand by their cars in this super space. For an even longer-term impact, you can add the names of these winning employees onto the sign that denotes this spot. By doing so, you have actually turned this sign into a trophy.

Epilogue

The chance of winning a special parking spot can drive people to work even harder.

24

Promotional Opportunities

One of the best ways to recognize and reward outstanding performance is to promote employees who consistently demonstrate excellence in their work. In many respects, promotion is the ultimate reward at work because it fulfills the successful employees' needs for recognition, achievement, responsibility, and personal growth. Employees also enjoy the more tangible rewards that typically accompany a promotion, such as a raise or a better office or workstation.

When promotions are carried out equitably, there are even rewards for employees who are not promoted. For example, it is rewarding for employees to see that the company promotes from within, and this can further energize them to work harder to receive a similar reward.

You can make a promotion even more rewarding by accompanying it with a formal announcement, a photo opportunity, and a personal note to the employee. Employees remember every promotion in their career, and these small steps make every promotion even more memorable.

Assignment

Look carefully at your employees and rate each on a scale from 1 to 10 in terms of promotability, with 10 being the best. For those who rank high, review the advancement opportunities in your department and company at large, and consider moving them up if possible. At the same time, meet with each employee at the lower end of the continuum and start designing a developmental program with them.

Epilogue
When you promote an employee, you are also promoting productivity, commitment, and motivation.

25

Keep Your Eye on the Wall

You can dramatically increase the positive impact of any reward by simultaneously providing some publicity. An outstanding way to do this is to designate one wall for employee recognition.

It can be called the "Wall of Fame," and there should be nothing on it except items that focus on employee rewards, recognition, and appreciation. This is where you would place photos, announcements, and commendations regarding your employees' outstanding work and accomplishments. The Wall should be in an area with a good deal of employee traffic, and employees should be able to stop and look at the postings without creating a bottleneck.

The Wall of Fame turns any single reward into a double reward. The first is the reward itself, and the second is having a photo and write-up on this wall. Employees sense high levels of recognition every time they see themselves on it, and the rewards keep coming when coworkers mention that they saw them on "the Wall."

Assignment

Take a tour of your offices, work area, or building and look for the perfect wall that can be transformed into the Wall of Fame. Once you have made your choice and lined up the necessary approvals, make sure the wall has its own unique color and an eye-catching graphic. Once it's ready, put the word out to all.

Epilogue

A Wall of Fame is the corporate equivalent to having one's name in lights.

26

A Polished Reward

One gleaming example of a highly visible reward that is consistently well received is a free carwash. When your team has been performing well and you are seeking a sweeping reward, this one really shines.

On a basic level, a newly washed car saves your employees time and money, two commodities that your employees truly value. In a broader sense, this reward tells your employees that you care about them whether they are on the job or off. Timing the carwash with the completion of a major project or the start of a new business cycle is an excellent way to psychologically wipe the slate clean and start fresh.

> ### *Assignment*
>
> Go to your favorite search engine and enter your geographical location and the words "mobile carwash." Check out each site and contact those that look best. You can negotiate prices, and be sure to check references. When the time arrives to book a date, try for a Friday. Employees love a shiny car for the weekend.

As employees go to and from work for days and possibly weeks after the carwash, the good feelings associated with this reward will be riding with them. And to keep this reward fair, don't forget to give carwash vouchers to employees who carpool or take public transportation to work.

> **Epilogue**
> *Giving your employees a free carwash is a great reflection on you and your company.*

27

What's Cooking?

If you are looking for a fun reward, you and some of your fellow managers should replace your managerial garb with chef's apparel and cook a meal for your employees. Some of the popular offerings include pancakes and eggs for breakfast, burgers and salads for lunch, or a pasta dinner.

On the one hand, this is a tasty way to say thanks to your employees for doing a great job. At the same time, when you are cooking up a meal for your employees, you are also cooking up opportunities for them to get to know you better. You may be a highly accessible and communicative manager, but when you sport an apron and a chef's hat, even the most miniscule barriers to communication fall by the wayside. Importantly, the lines of

Assignment

Meet with your fellow managers to discuss this reward and the logistics of applying it in your department or company. Select the meal that works best for all of you. A quick search online or in your local phone directory will help you line up all of the food, cooking equipment, silverware, plates, and other items needed to make this a very palatable reward.

communication that are opened at these meals tend to stay open long afterwards. These events not only reward your team, they build your team.

Epilogue

Cooking a meal for your employees gives them recognition they can savor, and that's food for thought.

28

Perfect for the Wall or Desk

When employees accomplish great feats, whether in terms of special projects, work beyond the call of duty, or meeting extra challenging goals, there are some traditional rewards that are still very popular. In this regard, trophies, plaques, ribbons, and certificates are among the most enduring rewards for outstanding performance.

These rewards are particularly compelling when they are personalized not only with the employee's name, but also with a few laudatory comments that

Assignment

Look at your employees who may be carrying out particularly demanding assignments and ask yourself if there are any who merit this type of reward. If so, contact a local or online award company and check out the offerings. When you find what you like, write a personalized inscription, place your order, and schedule the ceremony.

describe what he or she has done. If you want to raise the recognition a few decibels, give out these rewards in a ceremony. At such an event, speak glowingly of the employee's accomplishment, express your appreciation and congratulations, hand the award to him or her, and then pose for a photo for the Wall of Fame and company Website.

Employees typically put these awards in their offices, and a good piece of the satisfaction they felt on the day they received them will come back every time they glance at their trophy, plaque, or certificate.

Epilogue

Giving out traditional rewards can be a great tradition in your company.

29

Special Silly Trophies

If you are looking for a fun way to recognize and reward your employees, come up with an original trophy to honor performance on a specific project, program, or event. It can be anything you want—a rock, a dented can, an archaic cell phone, a used running shoe....

This trophy is typically passed from one winning individual or team to another. It adorns a desk or work area for a given amount of time and is then conferred to the next person or team that earns it.

Assignment

Look at your employees' projects on an individual and group basis, and try to find one that lends itself particularly well to this type of reward. Original trophies are especially enticing on projects that call for spirited competition within your team. Write down at least 10 trophy ideas, and then pick the one that looks like the most fun.

You can call these trophies whatever you wish. For example, perhaps there was an employee from yesteryear whose long hours and dedication greatly surpassed all others. You could name a trophy after this person and award it to the employee who demonstrates dedication and persistence far beyond the call of duty. This trophy could be a broken clock, as the winning employee obviously has no idea of the time.

Epilogue

A seemingly meaningless trophy can be a highly meaningful reward.

30

On the Spot

A spot bonus is one of the best ways to provide recognition and rewards right on the heels of desired behaviors. This is a reward that you immediately give to an employee when you catch him or her doing something terrific.

The bonus itself should not be visible to your employees until you see outstanding behavior. At that instant, pull it out of your pocket or purse and hand it to that employee. Be sure to offer hearty congratulations and thanks. If there are other employees around, that's even better.

This reward can be whatever works best for you and your employees, all the way from a cool gift certificate to cold cash. For maximum impact, be sure to place this reward in special wrapping that clearly designates what it is. This is a great way to build excitement, suspense, and tradition. When you give one of these bonuses, be sure to note it in the employee's file.

Epilogue

Spot bonuses are a great way to reduce spotty performance.

31

Table for Two

For your employees who are putting in extra long hours, one fulfilling reward is a dinner for two. However, this is more than simply picking a restaurant and then handing them a meal ticket.

If you want this to be a rewarding meal in all respects, pick out not only an excellent restaurant, but also one that your employee may have mentioned glowingly in the past. If he or she has not noted a restaurant by name, try to learn the kinds of foods he or she prefers and then make your choice. Rewarding your hard-working employees with dinner at the latest trendy eatery can be a big turkey if your employee does not like the food.

Assignment

Make a list of your employees and their favorite restaurants or foods. If you cannot come up with anything, it's time to spend more time getting to know your employees. When you see any of them repeatedly working extreme hours, hand them a certificate for that ideal meal.

Your hard-working employee probably missed a good number of dinners with his or her significant other, so be sure to include this individual as well. He or she plays a key role in your employee's life, and some thanks and recognition for this individual can make those long work hours a little more palatable.

Epilogue

Dinner for two is a perfect reward for employees who are literally and figuratively hungry.

32

Be a Sport

If you are looking for a healthy, exciting, and fun way to generate recognition for your employees, take a look at company-sponsored athletic teams. You can easily find leagues in most cities for such sports as bowling, soccer, softball, volleyball, and many more.

When employees are on a company athletic team, recognition comes from all over the lot. Employees on these teams get recognition every time the team does anything, starting with the team's formation and ending with its final game. This recognition also includes write-ups and photos on the company Website and Wall of Fame.

There is a great deal of recognition tossed back and forth among the players on these teams, and it is turbocharged when it comes from teammates who happen to be part of senior management. In fact, conversations among teammates often include more than sports, and they can easily open doors to choice assignments and opportunities.

> ### *Assignment*
>
> Contact your local parks and recreation department for information on company-sponsored teams in your area. Give your employees a summary of these programs, and then conduct a poll to see how many employees are interested playing any of these sports. Total it all up, select the most popular sport, put your name on the top of the list, and let the signups begin.

> ### Epilogue
> *Both on the field and off, being on a company team can be highly rewarding for all of the players.*

33

See a Sport

Tickets to sporting events are a terrific way to reward individual or group performance. If employees meet specific objectives, they are rewarded with tickets to a local sporting event, such as a baseball game.

Depending on the project and participants, these rewards can be given to a few employees or even the entire department. In fact, when you make this a group award, you are likely to see more team-oriented behaviors among the employees. You are also likely to hear the employees incorporate more sports vocabulary into their daily work as they strive to handle curveballs, play hardball, and avoid striking out.

> ### Assignment
> Look over the projects anticipated for the next few months and see if any lend themselves to this type of reward. If you find one, spell out the specific objectives, contact the closest professional sports organization and start lining up the tickets, and then present the project to your employees.

If they meet the goals and get to go to a ballgame, you can boost the recognition by giving them coupons for free food and beverages at the park. For some additional recognition, contact the ballpark ahead of time and have the employees' names flashed on the scoreboard for an official welcome.

Epilogue
While professional athletes stretch every day, your employees are likely to stretch when given the opportunity to win tickets to a game.

34
For the Sports

Assignment

If your employees are midway in a project right now and you would like to give them a rewarding boost, go to your friendly search engine and enter the words "promotional" and "logo." Look over the sports-oriented offerings and order some that your employees will enjoy. When the items arrive, have your ceremony, and be sure to set aside some time to roll up your sleeves and play.

In keeping with the theme of linking recognition and rewards to sports, there are some hands-on rewards in this area that work and play particularly well. These sporting rewards are long on fun, and they include items such as Nerf footballs, Frisbees, Koosh balls, golf balls, tennis balls, and kites.

These rewards should be handed out with overstated pomp and circumstance. If you would like them to have a longer-term impact, you can have your company name placed on them. And if you are giving out the item because of performance on a particular project or event, you should have that noted on it as well. Every time your employee plays with one of these rewards, even for years to come, the good feelings are rekindled every time the award is thrown, kicked, passed, or flown.

Epilogue

Employers and employees can score all sorts of points when the rewards are sports items.

35

A Great Pad

If you are looking for a different way for your employees to feel recognized and rewarded every time they sit down at their computers, one of the best is the personalized mouse pad. This is one of those fun rewards that you can give to your employees for their ability to work around computer glitches, squelch ridiculous e-mail, control the amount of mail stored in their inboxes, or successfully handle other techie problems.

This mouse pad should include the company name

Assignment

Look at the performance of your employees in terms of their ability to make the best use of their computers. If there are any who are a virtual cut above the others, they may be FIT employees. Make your selection, go to your choice search engine, enter the words "custom" and "mouse pad," and you'll find a mouse pad that is the perfect fit.

and logo, the employee's name, and the name of the reward. Perhaps these employees are designated as Friends of Information Technology, or FIT. These FIT employees should receive their pads at an over-the-top ceremony, followed by photos on the Website and Wall of Fame.

Whenever these employees boot up their computers, they will briefly flash back on the good times associated with this reward, and that is a great way to start any day.

Epilogue

In spite of their location, mouse pads are anything but underhanded rewards.

36

Let's Do Lunch Here

Assignment

Look over your employees on an individual and group basis to determine if any are about to reach an important objective. If so, check the calendars and set up an in-house lunch. Fridays are often the best days, and be sure to invite the entire department and senior management.

When your team or a key person on it meets an important goal or milestone, a casual and enjoyable way to reward and recognize the accomplishment is with light lunch right in the department.

The objective of these casual and light-spirited get-togethers is to focus attention on your deserving employees, rather than focusing on the food that is being served. As for the actual condiments, you can go as basic as pizza, sub sandwiches, or a deli platter. Or, if the honoree or honorees have a favorite food, then that should be the selection du jour.

As part of this event, be sure to take a few minutes to single out the individual or group and say a few laudatory words in front of all the attendees. You can make the experience even more significant for everyone by inviting some of the company's senior managers to attend and say a few words.

Epilogue

With a light celebratory lunch in the department, the most important items being served are recognition, attention, and appreciation.

37

Let's Do Lunch There

If you want to raise the stakes (and possibly the steaks) in these celebratory lunches for your employees, you should hold the event off-site at a local restaurant. You can personalize it by selecting an eatery that is preferred by the individual or team that you wish to recognize.

One major advantage of holding a recognition lunch off-campus is that there are fewer work-related interruptions and distractions, and this makes the honorees the center of attention. This also allows all of the employees to absorb the full impact of this type of recognition. In fact, not only do the honorees sense a high degree of recognition at these lunches, all of the employees who are invited to attend feel personally recognized as well.

51

Assignment

If the performance of any of your employees as individuals or groups merit this type of reward, or you anticipate that they will soon be doing so, contact some of the favorite local restaurants, check for a private or semi-private area, and make a reservation at the one that works best. When the time is right, you should have no reservations about announcing the lunch and inviting some senior managers to attend as well.

Epilogue

When you reward your employees with lunch at a favorite restaurant, the honorees sense that they are the real "specials of the day."

38

It's a Gas

Many studies are finding that gasoline prices are of major importance to growing numbers of employees. As a result, some of today's best rewards are gasoline gift cards. They look like plastic gift cards from any retailer, and they have a dollar amount right on the front, typically $25, $50, or $100.

Because rewards work best when they meet your employees' needs, gasoline gift cards certainly fit the bill. They clearly demonstrate that you looked carefully for a reward that your employees can actually use. While there certainly is a place for "warm and fuzzy" rewards, there is also a place for functional rewards, especially those that fill the employees' needs while also filling their gas tanks.

Your employees will sense a good deal of recognition when you hand them one of these cards, and they will relive some of

Assignment

One of the easiest ways to purchase these cards is online. Use any search engine and enter the words "gasoline" and "gift cards." You will quickly find all sorts of options for all sorts of prices. Select and order the cards you want, and when they arrive, start giving them out for excellent performance.

those positive feelings when they use their cards to fill up their cars and get back on the road.

Epilogue
Gasoline gift cards are fulfilling rewards that truly generate miles of smiles.

39

The Rewards of Carpooling

Even if you do nothing but encourage your employees to carpool, you are actually setting the stage for them to receive several inherent rewards. For example, carpooling allows them to travel in carpool lanes, save wear-and-tear on their cars, save money in gas and repairs, get to know some of their co-workers, experience less stress, and help the environment.

You can make this practice even more rewarding for carpoolers by adding some incentives such as special parking and free car washes, or you can go a step further and enter all of them, plus those who take public transportation, into a monthly drawing where they can win prizes such as movie tickets, supermarket gift cards, and, of course, gasoline gift cards.

Assignment

Send an e-mail to your employees announcing the carpool incentive program, and ask all who are interested to let you know. Review the names and addresses of those who respond, and let them know if there is a possible match. Be sure to inform all new employees about this program, as any new hire could be a perfect carpooling buddy for someone who is still driving solo. And don't forget to post the names of the employees in the winning carpools.

Epilogue

A carpool incentive program is a great vehicle for driving many of your company's messages home, and driving them to work as well.

40

Entertaining Ideas

When employees work extra long hours and complete a seemingly unending project, a rewarding way to put a period at the end of the sentence is to take them to see a movie, a play, or other entertainment during the day. On that day, bring your employees together as if you are holding a departmental meeting, and then surprise them by announcing that all of you will soon be leaving for something special.

You can tell them where they are going, or keep it a secret and let the excitement and suspense build along the way. And to make the travel more fun and memorable, the preferred mode of transportation is one or more limousines, although a bus will surely do. Try to select an event that is in great demand and has received rave reviews, and be sure the program ends in time for the employees to get back and leave work at a normal hour.

Assignment

If your employees will soon be wrapping up a highly demanding project, start scanning newspapers and online services for a special entertainment event as their reward. As soon as you lock in a completion date for the project, lock in tickets for the entertainment, and lock in the transportation, too.

Epilogue
When you reward your employees by taking them to entertaining events, they are more likely to entertain your ideas, inputs, and suggestions.

41

Try This on for Size

Apparel can be a very fitting reward for your employees. You can generate high levels of fun and recognition by giving out clothing, ranging from T-shirts or boxer shorts to pricier items such as designer ties and scarves. When a major project wraps up, you can also show up at work with hats, shirts, blouses, or sweatshirts; have a mini-ceremony; and give them out. These items are particularly popular when they include your company logo.

You can go even further in linking apparel to recognition by designating one particular item of clothing as the highest honor in your company. It can be given out for outstanding performance in any area that you desire, such as sales, cost reduction, community service, or employee development. This item, typically a very nice jacket, sweater, or hat, would have its own special color, and nothing like it should be given out by your company.

Assignment

Start building an inventory of apparel to give out when your employees deserve it. Look carefully at your employees to get an idea of the kind of clothing they prefer, and make sure that whatever you give is in line with the season. You can order the apparel at your favorite online or offline store, and you can use these same resources to emblazon the selections with your company logo.

> **Epilogue**
> *Recognizing and rewarding employees with apparel is a warm and fuzzy strategy that typically wears well with everyone.*

42

Greetings and Salutations

You have a great opportunity to provide recognition to your employees when you bring visitors through the department. Many managers stroll right through with the visitors in tow, but say nothing to the employees along the way. This actually means that the managers are showing the visitors nothing, because departments are nothing without the employees.

When a manager ignores the team in these situations, the message to the employees is that they are unimportant and insignificant. However, if you

> **Assignment**
>
> The next time you take a visitor through the department, set aside a few extra minutes for some meet-and-greet with your team. To build the recognition even further, think of something positive to say about your employees as you pass through their work areas.

simply say "hello" to your employees as you and your visitors amble by, the employees sense high levels of recognition and self-worth. And if you add the employees' names and even stop to make quick introductions and exchange a few words, their sense of personal recognition is even greater.

There will obviously be times when you and your visitors must rush through the department because of time constraints, but even then, a nod or a smile to your team can go a long way.

Epilogue

When you bring visitors through your department and say nothing, you are actually saying something quite negative. A minute of recognition can bring hours of satisfaction.

43

Stamps of Approval

Assignment

Look at your employees' performance, select a few individuals or a group that merit this recognition, and then take some photos with a digital camera. Just for fun, don't tell your employees why you are doing this. Go to an established site, such as stamps.com, and follow the prompts. Be ready with the camera when you give out these fun rewards.

One of the newest ways to recognize and reward your employees for outstanding performance is with U.S. postage stamps. You can now put photos of your employees on these stamps, and they can be used just like regular stamps.

This starts with a picture of whoever has merited recognition, whether it's an individual, group, or entire department. Once you have selected your favorite picture, go online to one of the many postage sites, upload the photo, crop it, add your own text, add the company logo if you wish, and then place your order. In a matter of days, the stamps will arrive at your office.

You can use these stamps on business correspondence, or you can give them to your employees for their own use. Either way, this is a highly personalized reward, and it is a great way to spread the word about your employees' excellent performance.

Epilogue

Personalized postage stamps literally go a long way toward recognizing your employees and pushing the envelope in this area.

44
A Message From the President

If you have an employee or group whose performance, accomplishments, or growth have been off the chart, one outstanding way to recognize and reward this achievement is with a personal note from the company president. The note should offer personalized congratulations for a particular success, along with encouragement to keep up the good work.

This message can be sent by e-mail or as a traditional letter. While both approaches will be well received, a traditional letter includes company letterhead and logo plus an original signature from the president. The aesthetics of this approach far outweigh e-mail, and an employee is likely to hold onto a letter for a long time. A letter is more likely to be framed than the same message via e-mail. This type of recognition can be even more compelling if the president personally delivers the letter and stays around for a few minutes to chat.

59

Assignment

Meet with the company president to set the stage for this type of recognition. Tell the president about any employees who are on the road to meriting this recognition, and ask for his or her thoughts as to who deserves this honor. When your employee or employees meet the objectives in question, contact the president immediately and put this recognition program in motion.

Epilogue

Personalized recognition from the company president is the highest form of corporate praise, and it places the employees on a high as well.

45

Hot Wheels

If you want to turbo-charge your recognition and reward program, give the best performer the use of powerhouse car for a couple of weeks or longer. Some of the cars of choice include the Porsche Boxster, BMW Z4, and Corvette.

This can be an appropriate reward in contests that have measurable results, such as those based on sales volume, dollars collected in credit, or number of units produced. You can also use this reward in programs that are not directly focused on productivity, such as a drawing for all employees who have not missed work or have been accident-free for a stipulated amount of time.

This reward also works well in broader recognition programs, such as by awarding the Employee of the Month with one of these cars for a month. Some companies actually own cars for this purpose, while others have lease or rental arrangements.

Assignment

Use your favorite online search engine, car dealership, or car broker to check out the costs of renting or leasing one of these cars. Once you find the best deal for your company, announce the program and be sure to include photos. When you give the keys to the employee, the ceremony should resemble the christening of a new jet, complete with throngs of applauding employees.

Epilogue

For a memorable reward that combines excitement, glamour, and pizzazz, try rewarding your employee's high performance with the use of a high-performance car.

61

46

I See Your Performance and I Raise You

For employees who consistently demonstrate outstanding performance, one of the best rewards is a raise. This is a great way to tell your employees that you are satisfied with their attainment of specific goals as well as their overall performance.

When you have employees who merit a raise, think carefully when determining the actual amount. A raise that is perceived as too low can be interpreted as an insult or a sign of dissatisfaction. And surprisingly, a raise that is too high can actually make employees feel uneasy and confused. An exorbitant increase in salary also raises the question of what you will do for an encore next year.

There is a great opportunity for compelling recognition right before the raise appears in an employee's paycheck. At that time, sit down with each such employee and express your satisfaction with his or her work and the pleasure you derive in giving the raise. Wrap up the session with the hope for more of these types of meetings in the future.

Assignment

Before providing any raises, it is important to not only review your employees' performance, but also to review your company's raise policies, practices, and standards; the financial plans and budgetary constraints; and how your company prefers to position its pay levels relative to other companies in your area.

> **Epilogue**
> *When you reward an employee with a raise, you are simultaneously raising employee satisfaction, motivation, morale, and commitment.*

47

Recognizing Your Employees and More

Your employees are not the only ones who make major sacrifices when job demands reach a boiling point. Many employees in the workplace cauldron have significant others who lose shared quality time during the crunch. When these crunches extend into months or longer, that loss changes from quality time to quantity time.

In addition to providing recognition and rewards to your employees during these periods, a thoughtful step is to provide some recognition for their significant others. You can do this by sending them a personal note of appreciation and thanks.

Along with the note, you should include a special gift, preferably something that your employee and his or her significant other can do together, such as dinner at a great restaurant, tickets to a play, or even a

Assignment

As you review each employee's performance during the periods of extremely extended hours, find out the name of his or her significant other, and then select a special gift they can share. As soon as you see a point where your employee can come up for air, send off the note and gift. And don't be surprised if you receive an even nicer note in return.

63

weekend cruise. Your employee will feel personally rewarded that you took a step to recognize this important person in his or her life.

Epilogue

When you recognize and reward a hard-working employee's significant other, you are sending a very significant message.

48

Here's a Suggestion

If you are looking for a way to generate amazing ideas for your department or company, and you are simultaneously looking for new opportunities to provide recognition and rewards, one approach that handily meets both of these goals is an Employee Suggestion Program. This is a program that solicits employee input, and then implements as many ideas as possible.

Today's suggestion programs include managerial support, a commitment to respond to every suggestion, as well as a commitment to implement any feasible idea. While some companies still use an old-fashioned suggestion box, many are now opting for an online suggestion system.

Either way, employees whose suggestions are implemented should be given predetermined rewards that can range from a percentage of the money a suggestion saves or earns, all the way to cash or special gifts befitting the occasion or suggestion. And regardless of the reward, it should always be presented in front of the employee's associates and members of senior management.

Assignment

Start the wheels turning today to set up an employee suggestion program. Tailor the program to fit your department or company, assemble a publicity package to announce it, set up an online or offline box, and finalize the kinds of rewards to be given out. Line up a buy-in from top management, and then launch the program.

Epilogue

In your quest for programs that recognize and reward employees, one helpful suggestion is an Employee Suggestion Program.

49

Post the Good Words

For those times when your employees demonstrate a behavior you really like and appreciate, you can provide some immediate, spontaneous, and impromptu recognition by writing a quick upbeat message on a Post-it or similar self-stick note, and then posting it right on the employee's door, desk, or even his or her monitor.

When you give this type of recognition, your message should be brief and positive in expressing thanks and appreciation for the employee's actions. Be sure to include the employee's name, and don't forget to sign yours.

There are Post-its or other self-stick notes in all sorts of sizes and colors, and you can vary these depending upon what your employee has done. You can even add more variety to the mix by including some with preprinted messages of thanks and congratulations. These messages tend to take on a special meaning as indicators of your satisfaction, and that gives them tremendous psychological value as sources of recognition.

Assignment

Assemble an inventory of self-stick notes of different sizes, colors, and preprinted messages. When an employee demonstrates a particularly positive behavior, write out and post one of these notes in his or her office or work area. You can compound the value of these notes by giving a gift coupon to a particular store, restaurant, or event to any employee who receives 20 of them.

Epilogue

Self-stick notes provide recognition that sticks around for a long time.

50

A New Newsletter

Whether you go with a traditional hard copy or a glitzy online edition, a company newsletter offers abundant opportunities to recognize and reward employees. While employees may read these publications to get a better idea of changes and developments in the company, their interest can be piqued and peaked if you include special stories and photos that feature them.

> **Assignment**
>
> Meet with your fellow managers to discuss the publication of a company newsletter. Bring in online and hard copy samples, and let the group decide on the format and division of labor. Encourage your employees to take a role, because one excellent source of recognition comes from authoring an article.

When your employees leap over hurdles and grab the corporate brass ring of success, you can use a newsletter to spread the word to the entire company. If there have been ceremonies to recognize the accomplishment, a write-up and some photos in the newsletter can make the positive feelings even more long-lasting.

You should also have a feature in the newsletter that singles out an employee or team for special recognition, and the criteria can be whatever you want, such as goal attainment, volunteer work, or lowest absenteeism. To build interest, excitement, and suspense, no one should know who is in this section until the newsletter is distributed.

Epilogue

A company newsletter can help a recognition program break out of its old mold, and that's a breaking story.

51

Stop the Presses

If you are looking for wider recognition for your employees, your local newspaper can be a great place to air their accomplishments, achievements, and successes. Some of the great things your employees do are indeed news, whether on the job or off, and they can make excellent stories either in the business section or as a piece for a human interest columnist. In addition, some business sections intermittently run columns that announce promotions and other employee developments, and that could be a perfect spot for this recognition.

For the employee or employees who are named, the pride and excitement will be practically palpable. After all, this is recognition from

> **Assignment**
>
> Look at recent accomplishments of your employees and see if any jump off the page. If you find even one, put together some notes, contact your local paper, and ask for the reporter or columnist who covers this kind of story. In addition, because some newspapers have columns that invite readers to submit their own newsworthy stories, you can try this as an alternative strategy.

you and the community at large. Interestingly, the rest of your employees are going to feel almost as proud simply by working with whoever is lauded in the paper.

Epilogue

When employees see their names in the news, the lines stay in their heads for a long time, giving an entirely new and important meaning to the word "headlines."

52

Add Recognition With Ads

Another way that the media can generate recognition for your employees is through advertising. You can purchase an ad of practically any size in business sections of most newspapers as well as in most trade magazines. These ads can provide eye-catching praise, appreciation, and recognition to individual employees or groups of employees for their outstanding accomplishments and success.

This type of recognition is particularly appropriate and effective when employees have stellar sales or productivity over a predetermined period of time. You can also use this form of recognition when employees

Assignment

Be on the lookout for these types of announcements in local papers and trade journals. Build a file of these ads, and be ready to put one together when one of your employees merits this type of recognition. Contact the newspapers and journals to get their pricing, and contact framers in your area to get their pricing to have the ad framed.

are promoted to senior levels or when they complete major projects or deals. Ads also work well for recognizing an employee or group of employees that has been previously honored by another institution or organization for excellent contributions, such as for voluntarism at a community center or hospital.

Epilogue

A congratulatory advertisement sends a positive message about the employee or employees being honored, and it sends an equally positive message about your company.

53

Use Your Headlines

While most newspapers are not likely to place your employees' accomplishments in the front-page headlines, there is a fun way for you to do so. There are many companies that will take a generic front page of a newspaper and print any headline you would like.

These fake headlines are a creative way to recognize employees for some of their unique successes along the way. For example, if the company's athletic team wins a key game or loses a heartbreaker, or an employee generates the most recyclable paper, you can have headlines humorously describe the event.

The best time to deliver these newspapers is during an informal celebration, such as a pizza lunch. Be sure to have someone with a camera ready to capture the moment as your employees proudly display their front-page story.

Assignment

Make a note of your employees who have just reached or are about to reach a fun milestone, and then write some pithy headlines for these accomplishments. Use any major search engine and enter the words "headline," "gag," and "fake," and you'll see several companies that are ready to place your personalized headline in bold print on the front page of a generic newspaper. Place your order and set a date to celebrate.

Epilogue
Fun headlines can put you at the head of the line when it comes to providing creative and innovative recognition.

54

Executive Dining

A powerful way to recognize your employees and simultaneously improve communication, morale, and productivity, is to invite the company president or another topsider to have an informal on-site lunch with the employees every month. These can be light lunches, because the most important item for the employees to digest is information.

These lunches are an opportunity for the senior manager to present information on important trends, developments, and plans for the company, as well as to discuss the employees' input and answer their questions.

Assignment

Meet with the president or a senior manager with your company (and either one could be you), review the benefits of this monthly session, and put this program in place. The best days are usually the last Friday of each month, but this can vary dependent on issues specific to your company and industry. Put the event on the calendar, and put the word out to the employees.

On one level, the employees appreciate being kept up-to-date and exchanging ideas with senior management, while on a deeper level this type of dialogue tells the employees that management regards them as highly valued resources whose ideas, input, and suggestions are critical to the company's success.

Epilogue

When a company president or topsider has an informal monthly lunch with the employees, it is a recognition booster-shot that helps immunize the employees for such corporate ailments as alienation, boredom, and frustration.

55

Peer-to-Peer

While recognition from you and other topsiders can go a long way, recognition from coworkers can hit home as well. This type of feedback is particularly meaningful because coworkers often know more about what an employee is doing, feeling, experiencing, and accomplishing than an employee's manager.

An excellent way to generate this type of recognition is to hold an employee meeting totally devoted to peer feedback, and the only ground rule is that all such feedback must be focused on their fellow employees' accomplishments, strengths, and contributions. Each employee should write out these positive comments in advance on 3 × 5 cards, with one card for each of their coworkers.

Assignment

Set a date for this meeting, tell your employees about this program, and then give them a set of cards. Try to have the meeting room set up with all of the chairs in a circle with nothing in the middle. With all of the chairs in a circle, the meeting has an egalitarian atmosphere, perfect for peer-to-peer recognition.

At the meeting, you should read all of the cards for each employee, and the group members can add any comments they wish. When the meeting ends, you should give each employee his or her stack of cards. The recognition associated with this event is long lasting, and it is reinforced when employees look back over their cards.

Epilogue

Providing recognition to peers is rewarding to the givers as well as the receivers.

56

Happy Anniversary

No matter how often you provide recognition, each employee has one special day when he or she should always be recognized, namely his or her anniversary with the company. By congratulating your employees when they reach these annual milestones, you are providing them with appreciation and recognition for an entire year's worth of work, commitment, and performance. This type of recognition makes them feel more positive about all they have accomplished during this period, and it sets the stage for continued successful performance.

In addition, as the years increase, so should the recognition. For example, employees who reach their five-year anniversary should have a luncheon where they are given a framed plaque and a special reward, such as dinner at a great restaurant. With each five-year increment, the celebration and rewards should be more and more elaborate.

Assignment

Check your employees' starting dates and mark your calendar right now so that you congratulate each on his or her next anniversary. For employees who are about to reach five- or 10-year anniversaries, set up the celebrations. And if you have any employees who have already reached or passed these landmarks, be sure to include them in the ceremony and give them plaques and special rewards retroactively.

> ### Epilogue
> *When you formally recognize employees on their anniversary dates, you are helping them feel better about all they have given to the company and all the company has given to them.*

57

Savvy About Sabbaticals

An occasional day off can be very rewarding, so just think of the impact a few months off with pay, namely, a sabbatical, would have. This can be a perfect reward for employees who reach long-term milestones with your company, such as a 10th anniversary.

A sabbatical is the ultimate way to recognize and reward employee loyalty and performance. With growing numbers of employees seeking a better balance between work lives and personal lives, a sabbatical provides a unique opportunity for employees to spend quality time and quantity time with the significant others and significant interests in their personal lives.

Assignment

Look over your employees' tenure and note those who may be approaching 10- or 15-year anniversaries. Review the costs of a three-month sabbatical for these individuals, and consider a sabbatical of shorter duration if necessary. Either way, if the numbers work, select the employees who qualify, look carefully at coverage during their absence, pick the best time for these individuals to be out, and then launch the program.

When employees take off this amount of time, they not only relax and recharge their batteries, they also clear their heads of corporate cobwebs that may have been limiting their perspective and restricting their ability to think outside the box. As a result, they return to work feeling reenergized, reinvigorated, and rewarded.

Epilogue

A sabbatical that lasts a quarter of the year provides thanks and recognition for many quarters and in many quarters.

58

When Opportunity Knocks

Opportunities to recognize and reward employees occasionally fall into a manager's lap. For example, an employee wants to talk about something that has made him or her particularly proud. It might be part of a project, but it could just as easily be a piece of art created by the employee's child or a vacation photograph.

In these instances, some managers offer a perfunctory, "That's nice." At that point, the employee instantly senses that the manager is

Assignment

Think back on recent situations in which some of your employees approached you and proudly described an action or item, but your reaction was a little too blasé. Go back to these employees and ask to see the artwork, photograph, or whatever it was that led them to approach you in the first place. Give the item some genuine attention, and the employee some genuine recognition.

uninterested in any of this, and is therefore uninterested in the employee.

When an employee approaches you and speaks proudly of something he or she has accomplished or brought to work, you should get involved. If there is something to see, go see it; if there is something to read, go read it; if there is something to hear, go listen. Your employee is asking for recognition, and it's important for you to recognize that fact.

Epilogue

You can spend time looking for opportunities to recognize and reward employees, but don't forget that these opportunities are also looking for you.

59
Knocking Around for Opportunities

In addition to seizing the recognition opportunities that wander into your life, you can seize even more by doing some wandering yourself. By wandering around each day, you can find numerous recognition opportunities.

When you walk into your employees' offices, workstations, or work areas, keep all of your senses fine tuned, and the opportunities for recognition will jump out at you. You might spot new photos, certificates, or artifacts, or you might hear about the most recent accomplishments of your employees' significant others.

You can easily engage your employees in conversation about these positive developments, and these discussions in and of themselves are forms of recognition. However, by adding genuine words of praise, credit, or appreciation, you are providing your employees with instant, spontaneous, and personalized recognition that will leave them feeling pleased, proud, and pumped up.

Assignment

Plan to walk through your entire work area every day. You should acknowledge all of your employees, and spend a few minutes talking with some of them, but not the same employees every day. Try to discover those special accomplishments or developments that merit extra recognition, and then provide it.

Epilogue

When it comes to finding opportunities to recognize your employees, if you look around, you'll see that they are all around.

60

The Employees Are Entitled

One of the most important ways to recognize an employee's performance, productivity, and contributions is with a job title. Although it is understood that a job title defines a person's job, it is important to emphasize that the title plays a role in defining the jobholder.

Assignment

Look over individual performance levels in your department and consider adding some new and more accurate titles to reward employees who have clearly surpassed all expectations. In addition, consider placing such words as "lead," "senior," and "executive" in front of existing titles. During the next round of reviews, make all of the title adjustments as warranted by performance.

The various roles that people play in life serve to define them at various times. For example, there are roles as a father, mother, brother, sister, friend, coach, and numerous others. However, because working people tend to spend the majority of their waking hours on the job, the job title plays a key role in self-definition.

If you have an employee who has consistently stepped up and performed beyond the call of his or her job description, upgrading his or her title can be a durable, visible, and greatly appreciated form of recognition.

Epilogue

When you upgrade employees' titles, you also upgrade their self-esteem, satisfaction, and even their performance. Remember that people often perform up to the level of their titles.

61

Featured Employees

A unique way to recognize your employees as individuals and as teams is to feature them in company publications and literature. When you use photos of employees in advertisements, annual reports, new employee brochures, and company pamphlets, you send some very positive messages.

The opportunity to be in a company publication tells your employees that management is proud of them and views them as exemplifying what the company truly represents. In addition, when these types of photos are used in promotional literature, another message to the employees is that the company does not need to bring in glitzy or glamorous outsiders, thus avoiding the implication that the employees fall short in this regard. Employees feel proud simply to be asked if they would like to be photographed for these publications, and when they spot photos of themselves in them, they feel like stars. And that is appropriate, because they are your stars.

Epilogue

When you use candid photos of employees in the company's publications, the positive impact lasts longer than the publication itself; hence creating a new and important usage of the term "photographic memory."

62

Significant Others

Another great way to reward your employees is to recognize the significant events, milestones, and achievements of some of the significant others in their lives. These significant others include spouses, children, parents, partners, and even in-laws, and their accomplishments and milestones can include graduations, promotions, major birthdays, plus any honors they receive.

You can turn any of these events into a recognition moment by sending a congratulatory note to the employee, posting congratulations on the company Website or Wall of Fame, and sending a congratulatory note to the significant other.

When you recognize the accomplishments of people who are of primary importance in your employees' lives, you are providing indirect recognition to your employees, and this makes them feel proud. And this type of recognition further demonstrates and reinforces your commitment to a work-life balance.

Assignment

Keep an ear out for significant happenings in the lives of your employees' significant others. When you hear one, tell the employee you would like to send a note and post the accomplishment on the company Website and bulletin board. Once you do this, send an e-mail asking all of your employees to let you know about these kinds of accomplishments by their significant others so they too can be recognized.

81

Epilogue

When you recognize your employees' significant others for their achievements, events, and milestones, you are creating a warmer family atmosphere at work and at home.

63

Holiday Happenings

The major holidays provide a perfect setting and opportunity for you to ramp up recognition for your employees. For example, the Fourth of July is a great time for a company picnic. The event can be coordinated by a team of employees, which is a rewarding experience for them, while the picnic itself is rewarding for all of your employees.

Employees genuinely appreciate receiving turkey certificates at Thanksgiving, as well as a winter event to celebrate Christmas, Chanukah, and Kwanza. The format is up to you, your employees, and your budget. And a costume party and contest during the lunch hour on Halloween is a fun and low-cost way for the employees to generate some unique recognition for themselves.

Assignment

Look at your calendar for the coming year and select the holidays on which you would like to have special events. Put together a budget and then ask for employees to volunteer to be on the committee to stage the event. On the day of the event, be sure to single out these employees for special recognition.

When companies let these holidays slide by without a shred of recognition, many employees take it personally. And when you build some attention and recognition around these holidays, the employees take that personally…and positively.

Epilogue

Recognition should never take a holiday when the holidays arrive.

64

Give the Employees a Hand, Literally

Assignment

Look at the projects and performance of all of your employees. If you see any employees who have hit the wall or are about to do so, offer a positive and supportive helping hand. For future reference, take a look at the projects you are assigning to the members of your team, review their past performance on similar projects, and consider making some adjustments for those who are being constantly overwhelmed.

Regardless of your line of work, there can be projects that are so overwhelming for your employees that they truly need help. You can wait for employees to come up for air and ask you, but if you are managing by wandering around, you are going to see and hear the problem quite easily.

When you spot it, you should approach your employees and offer your help. Your employees will instantly sense some personal recognition because you think enough of them

83

to roll up your sleeves and work side by side with them. Doing so is a true vote of confidence for them.

Working directly with your employees is also going to give you more insight into their motivations, styles, standards, and objectives. This type of information can be very valuable as you seek additional ways to recognize and reward their performance in the future.

Epilogue
When you step in to help your employees, they often step up their performance to help themselves.

65
Give Your Employees a Hand, Figuratively

Another fun way to recognize your employees is to give them a hearty round of applause when they complete a particularly grueling, demanding, and draining assignment. While the sound of one person clapping does not typically echo through the hallways, a hearty round of applause from you as their manager will echo in their minds for quite a long time. And if you can round up a few other managers who have been directly or indirectly involved in the project, so much the better.

This round of applause is actually a standing ovation, one of the highest forms of recognition, respect, and psychological reward that one person can bestow on another.

When employees receive a round of applause from their manager or managers, they can only smile. That smile comes from a combination of pride, the fun of the moment, and the deep sense of recognition and gratification that their performance was truly noticed and appreciated.

Assignment

If you have one employee who just con-
quered a particularly monstrous project, you and
any other managers involved with this project
should get together and spontaneously walk into
the employee's office or workstation, say nothing, and just give him or her a round of applause.
From that point, you are on your own, and your
employee is on cloud nine.

Epilogue

*Without saying a word, a standing ovation for out-
standing performance can say more than many long-winded
orations.*

66

It's About Time

Another great way to recognize and reward your employees is to provide some flexibility in their work hours. Obviously,
this depends upon several issues, especially the employees' performance and the interdependence of their responsibilities.

Depending on these parameters, a flextime program can be very rewarding for all of the players. Such programs typically provide a band of time during which employees must be at work, while varying the times they can arrive and leave. Employees appreciate the flexibility, and they also appreciate management's recognition of their individuality and work-life balance.

Another aspect of this timely approach is to introduce telecommuting that allows employees to work from home. This does not have to be an all-or-nothing program, because you can structure it to let the employees telecommute as frequently or infrequently as you wish, all dependent upon the needs of your business and department.

Assignment

Review the roles, responsibilities, and performance of your employees, as well as the need for them to be physically present at your workplace each day. If you determine that flexibility is merited and poses no operational problems, introduce a pilot program that gives your employees some freedom regarding arriving and departing times over the next three months. At the end of this period, review the performance data and you should have no difficulty regarding the future of this program.

Epilogue

When you provide flexibility in the employees' work times, the employees feel rewarded many times over.

67

Go for the Goal

There's no question that having goals is motivational, and the internal and external recognition associated with achieving one's goals is particularly uplifting. You can set the stage for these compelling forms of personal recognition and psychological rewards by working with your employees to establish goals, and then providing coaching and guidance along the way.

However, it is important to make sure that your employees' goals are real goals, and not merely dreams. A real goal is clear, specific, prioritized, and measurable, and it includes a deadline date and benchmark dates along the way.

By devoting time to work directly with your employees to create their goals, you are telling your employees that their potential contribution to the organization is of great value. And, on a subtle level, you are telling your employees that they are of great value.

> **Epilogue**
> *It is clear that recognition comes from goal-getting, but it comes from goal-setting, too.*

68

Let's Do Lunch

When you give your employees an opportunity to spend some quality time with you alone, you are creating an opportunity for some quality recognition for them. One of the best ways to do this is to have a one-on-one lunch with each member of your team at least once every quarter.

This should be an off-site lunch at one of the better restaurants in your area. The topics can be whatever you and your employee desire, be it business, brainstorming, or baseball.

Assignment

Review your employees' calendars over the next two months and set up a lunch with each member of your team. Because you are the organizer, you should make the reservation, do the driving, and, of course, pay the bill. If your employee has a favorite nearby restaurant, you can personalize this recognition even more by going there.

Simply inviting an employee for lunch implies a high degree of appreciation, recognition, and interest from you. In this way, the recognition starts well ahead of the lunch itself. When you spend this time chatting with your employee and truly listening to whatever he or she is saying, your employee is going to walk away from this meal feeling proud, important, and respected, and these feelings are among the most meaningful rewards you can provide.

Epilogue

Most employees are hungry for recognition, and one-on-one lunches are a great way to satisfy this appetite.

69

Bottled-Up Rewards

Assignment

Look over the performance and style of your employees, and if you have one or two who are ready to receive some fun recognition, go to your favorite search engine and enter the words "personalized," "label," "water," and "wine." Be ready with graphics, a photo, and words of recognition, and then just follow the prompts. This type of reward is best served in front of others.

When your employees perform extremely well and you want to toast their excellence, try doing so with bottles of wine or water. And for that extra impact, you should go with a case. While the congratulatory nature of wine has been well established over the millennia, one might wonder about water's role in this activity.

As you might suspect, there is a catch. You can buy water and wine today with labels that you can personalize with graphics and your employee's name, photo, and any comments you wish.

By personalizing a reward in this way, the bottles of wine and water take on a broader meaning. On one level, it is simply fun for an employee to see his or her picture on these bottles, along with words of high praise. On a slightly different level, this reward demonstrates that you want to give your employees something special and help them feel like a special something.

Epilogue

When you reward your employees with bottles of water or wine adorned with personalized labels, they will drink it up.

70

Surveys Serve All

It is highly rewarding for employees at all job levels to have opportunities to present their opinions and suggestions on issues and developments in their department as well as in the company at large. While you can generate this type of input and the recognition that goes with it by being accessible, visible, and responsive to your employees, you can complement these positive outcomes on a regular and formalized basis through employee opinion surveys.

Surveys are anonymous online or offline questionnaires that typically have a combination of multiple choice and open-ended questions that focus on the employees' likes, dislikes, and suggestions. There are plenty of generic surveys available, along with professional services that can help you develop, conduct, and score them.

There is a good deal of recognition associated with simply participating in the survey process, and a great deal of recognition associated with changes and improvements that are made as a result.

Epilogue

Employee surveys ask many questions, but there is no question that they generate valuable information, improvements, and recognition.

71

The Value of Video

A growing number of companies are making short videos that feature their employees, and one of the clearest outcomes is that employees literally view them as a source of recognition.

The video itself can be a professional production or it can be handled internally. While the professionals can do a professional job, many companies today have would-be filmmakers who can use today's affordable cameras and technology to make a great video. And if the video is made by members of your team, they are in line for even more recognition.

The idea of the video is for the filmmakers to wan-

Assignment

Tell your employees that you are interested in having a company video, and see if any would-be filmmakers step up. If they do, look at samples of their work. Depending on what you see, you may want to check out some of the corporate filmmakers on the Internet. Either way, be sure to clarify objectives, content, style, budgets, and deadlines.

der around the company, camera in hand, and shoot unscripted footage of employees at work or at watercoolers, and catch a few of them for spontaneous comments. This video can be used for conferences, orientation programs, board meetings, or other events that draw customers, vendors, family, or guests into your offices. However, the first screening should be for all of your employees.

Epilogue
When it comes to corporate videos, employees enjoy the recognition associated with being in the spotlight.

72

Rewards for Referrals

If you bring your employees into the recruitment process and provide rewards and recognition for referring solid candidates to the company, you are generating more than the classic win-win outcome. You are generating a win-win-win outcome.

> ### **Assignment**
>
> If you do not have a formal reward program for employee referrals, put one in place today. It's basically a matter of coming up with the dollar amount, the length of time at work before the reward is granted, and some documentation for the referring employee to complete. If you already have such a program, tell the employees about it again, because these programs typically need booster shots.

The company wins because you are hiring strong candidates at a fraction of typical recruiting costs. The second winner is the applicant because he or she gets a job.

Winner number three is the employee who made the referral. This employee should be given a cash award after the new hire has remained with the company for a predetermined period of time, such as three months. Depending on the job level, the reward can be $100 to $500.

In addition, when you hire individuals recommended by your employees, you are showing your high level of respect for their judgment, and this makes all of the other rewards even sweeter.

> ### Epilogue
> *Having friends is rewarding, and working with them can be even more rewarding when there is a referral program.*

73

Mentors Mean More

It is clear that mentoring programs are an excellent way to enhance employee development, but it is important to add that these programs are also excellent sources of recognition.

When management provides employees with a mentor, one immediate message is that management truly cares about the employees and their success. With a mentor, management is making an extra effort to help the employees learn, grow, and achieve, and employees view this as a highly rewarding vote of confidence in their skills, abilities, and potential.

Assignment

Look for the new hires and others who are not performing up to par, and look for employees who are doing well and are often approached by others for advice and help. These latter employees are the natural leaders who should be considered for mentoring roles. Offer them the opportunity plus a pay increase, and, if they accept, assign them to mentor struggling employees and new hires.

In addition, because of the one-on-one nature of mentoring, a mentor utilizes one of today's most important educational concepts, namely training that is tailored to the individual's learning style. This leads to accelerated learning, success, and the recognition and rewards that soon follow. A mentoring program is also rewarding to the mentors because they typically receive considerable recognition, along with extra pay.

Epilogue

Mentors are in the unique position to give and receive recognition at the same time.

74

Creative Teams

Every company has issues, concerns, and problems that call for attention and resolution, but are never adequately assigned or addressed. For example, policies on sick leave may be outdated, some work areas can be too hot or too cold, supplies are in short supply, or there is too much internal e-mail.

There is a proven way to generate excellent solutions to these matters while simultaneously generating an excellent opportunity for employee recognition. These kinds of lingering problems are perfect targets for a task force of employees to address, analyze, and resolve. When employees are invited to do so, they appreciate the recognition associated with being invited onto the problem-solving team, as well as the appreciation that management provides when the project is successfully completed.

Assignment

Look for any lingering issues that have slid down the priority list but still need resolution. Pick the most important one and invite a diverse mix of employees to be on a team to correct it. Meet periodically with the team to make sure the members are on track in terms of timing, content, and budget. When the project is completed, set aside time at a meeting or gathering that includes many employees and then congratulate each member of this task force.

Epilogue

When employees are part of a team that solves a long-lasting problem, they typically receive long-lasting recognition.

75

Pre-hire Presence

If you want to make better hiring decisions and simultaneously generate recognition for your employees, one of the best strategies is to include them in the process of screening job applicants. It is particularly rewarding for employees to play this kind of role, because it is clear validation of their competence, professionalism, and judgment skills.

Assignment

The next time you are interviewing applicants, bring the best ones back to be interviewed by some of your employees. Pick two or three of your best employees to do the interviewing, and remind them to keep all of their questions job-related, focus on the applicant's work history, and throw in some work sample questions.

Research consistently shows that employers make better hiring decisions when applicants are interviewed by different members of the team. While you certainly have insight into what is needed for success in the company, your employees often have their own insight into the criteria for success, and when their insights are combined with yours, a better decision is made.

Your employees should interview candidates whom you have already screened and approved to go to the next step. Once your employees have completed these interviews, you should meet with them to discuss their findings. And, for this process to work, you should carefully consider what they say.

Epilogue

Better employees can recognize better applicants, and they feel personally recognized when asked to do so.

76

Flower Power

A visually captivating way to reward an employee who has really blossomed is to give him or her a bunch of colorful flowers. This type of recognition is an upbeat and lively way to let an employee know that you see and appreciate his or her growth.

Assignment

If you have an employee who has made great strides recently, give him or her a bunch of flowers, and attach a special gift or gift card to the arrangement. Plants have a good deal of greenery, so you might want to put something green in the envelope with the gift card.

Because of their beauty and fragrance, flowers continue to let an employee relive the good feelings associated with this recognition for many days to come. In addition, flowers in an office are an instant attention-grabber, and every person who walks into the employee's office or workstation is likely to say something about them, which leads to even more positively charged emotions.

If you want to attach a longer-term spin and reward onto this recognition, try using something other than a rubber band to hold the bunch of flowers together. For example, a watch or a belt can hold a bunch of flowers together quite nicely.

Epilogue
Flowers touch all of an employee's senses, and this literally makes flowers a very sensible reward.

77

In the Employee's Name

If you are looking for a way to provide meaningful recognition and rewards while helping the community at the same time, you should make a donation to a charity, organization, or institution in the name of your employee or employees. These types of donations are an important way to align your sense of generosity, altruism, and thoughtfulness with that of your employees.

> ### *Assignment*
>
> Let your employees know that you would like to make donations to their favorite charity or organization. Once you have a list of the suggested recipients, use it the next time you wish to commemorate a particularly meaningful and distinct accomplishment.

This is a perfect step to take when your employee or team has reached an important milestone or received an honor or distinction, whether provided by the company or an outside organization.

When you make this type of donation, the employees receive recognition from several quarters. Obviously, they sense recognition from you, and they also receive thanks and recognition from the entity that they designated to receive the donation. Additional recognition comes from the significant others in their work life and personal life who learn about the donation.

> ## Epilogue
> *When your employees deserve some recognition, consider a donation to a deserving organization.*

78
Early to Close

A great way to recognize and reward your employees is to close a little early before holiday weekends and midweek holidays. While this depends in part on workload demands and the nature of your business and industry, there are some real advantages associated with letting employees leave early.

However, it is important to note that leaving early does not necessarily mean taking the whole afternoon off. Even if you let your employees go an hour earlier, the gesture will be appreciated. When you take this type of action, you are rewarding your employees for their hard work, and you are also showing your understanding of their needs, interests, and responsibilities outside of work.

Assignment

If there is no business reason for remaining open regular hours before holidays and holiday weekends, and your employees have been operating at peak performance, close up early. Be sure to tell the employees that you are taking this action because they have been working so hard, and you will try to close early in the future if they continue to perform well.

100

> **Epilogue**
> *When you close up early before major holidays, you open up major recognition for your employees.*

79

Coffee, Tea, and Treats

When employees work hard, they enjoy taking a break to grab a cup of something and a snack. When these offerings match their tastes, employees view them as rewards. In fact, some employees work hard on a section of a project and promise to treat themselves to the coffee bar or vending machine as soon as they finish.

The offerings depend in great part on the company's finances and physical plant. Some companies are only able to provide vending machines, while others can have complete coffee bars and gourmet snacks. The key step is to provide the best that your company can afford.

> **Assignment**
>
> Ask your employees for their opinions and suggestions regarding the beverages and snacks offered at your company. Review the feasibility of upgrading your offerings in this area in accordance with their inputs. You can turn all of this into a greater recognition opportunity by forming an employee task force to study the matter and make some recommendations.

People have basic needs, such as for food, and they have higher-level needs, such as for recognition. An employer who

101

provides employees with beverages and snacks that they truly enjoy is in the unique position to satisfy basic and higher level needs at the same time.

Epilogue

Providing employees with their favorite coffees, teas, and treats is a tasteful way to reward hard work.

80

Degrees of Freedom

Growing numbers of employers are finding that scholarships for the employees' children are an excellent way to recognize loyalty and commitment from the employees while recognizing excellent performance from their children. Such scholarships tell your employees that they have done great work both on and off the job, and they again show your appreciation for the long hours that your employees have spent at work. It truly is rewarding for your employees to sense that you are partnering with them to help their children.

You can administer the scholarship program with a team of other managers, or you can select an outside foundation or association to administer it for you. With awards that can range from a few hundred dollars to several thousand dollars, these scholarships provide financial and psychological rewards for everyone involved.

Assignment

Enter the words "employee," "scholarship," and "plan" into your search engine and you will find resources to help you draft a scholarship plan. You should then meet with your company's tax advisor to finalize it. With the plan in place, invite the employees' children who meet the specifications to apply. Once the winners have been selected, be sure to provide them and their parents with plenty of recognition.

Epilogue

When you provide scholarships for your employees' children, you are providing recognition that lasts lifetimes.

81

Day Care for the Little Ones

One of the primary issues on the minds of numerous employees in today's workplace is childcare. Today's best companies recognize this reality and take action to deal with it, and you can, too. If your company has the financial wherewithal and the available workspace, it is worthwhile to consider developing an onsite day-care center for your employees' little ones. If this is too tall an order, another option is to work out a financial arrangement with a nearby first-rate day-care center.

Assignment

Meet with your employees to assess their interest in having childcare subsidized by the company. Because the on-site option is a major project that will require study over time, the key step from this point is to check out the day-care centers in your area, select the best, and meet with the owners to put together a joint program.

Regardless of the option you select, your actions have a strong undercurrent of recognition. By subsidizing childcare, you are rewarding your employees with a tangible benefit, and you are also recognizing their needs, keeping your commitment to work-life balance, and building an atmosphere of respect, trust, and support.

Epilogue

By taking care of day care, the attention that your employees would have focused on childcare matters can now be focused on work matters, and that really matters.

82

Convenience of a Concierge

One of the newest items on the recognition menu is a company concierge. A concierge at the workplace is a service you can retain to take care of many tasks, chores, and basic responsibilities that your hardworking employees are typically too busy to handle, such as personal shopping, picking up and dropping off dry cleaning, waiting for the cable repairperson at an employee's house, making dinner reservations, getting tickets to a special event, getting shoes repaired or polished, doing the marketing, taking a car to be serviced or washed, returning videos, and much more.

These services save time, reduce stress, and add great convenience to your employees' lives, giving them more freedom both on and off the job. A related benefit is that when these types of chores are lifted from your employees' shoulders, their productivity and satisfaction increase.

Assignment

Enter the words "corporate," "concierge," and the name of your city into a search engine and you will be led to any number of concierge companies that are literally at your service. Because many have an array of plans to suit your needs, you should review them carefully, go over their pricing, check their references, and then give the highest rated company a try.

Epilogue

Corporate concierge services provide your employees with one of life's greatest and most precious rewards: the gift of time.

83

Getting in Shape

With growing numbers of employees interested in toning their muscles, losing a few pounds, building their endurance, lowering their blood pressure, and simply taking better care of themselves, more employers are providing health-club memberships. Employees who work long hours can let themselves fall out of shape. Many are quick to say they should join a gym, but few do. This changes when the company rewards them with membership.

In addition, employers are becoming more aware of the fact that the health of their employees has a major impact on productivity, insurance premiums, and overall attitudes and morale, and health-club membership can help here, too.

Assignment

Use a telephone directory or search engine to find health clubs in your area. Visit each of them, check out the facilities and services, speak with a sales representative, and then select the club that offers the best program for your team. Try to find a club that has multiple facilities so that employees can exercise near their homes if they prefer.

This type of reward tells your employees that you see their health and the company's health as being inextricably intertwined. As employees take advantage of the health club's offerings, their appreciation of this form of recognition grows with each additional lap, curl, stretch, and dive.

Epilogue
Rewarding employees with a health-club membership makes them stronger and makes your company stronger, too.

84
Voluntary Recognition

You can create enormously meaningful recognition opportunities by encouraging employees to spend some time in volunteer activities. Voluntarism has become so important today that some employers are giving their employees a week or more off with pay so they can do volunteer work in their communities.

Volunteers are gladly welcomed in a broad range of organizations and institutions such as homeless shelters, schools, youth programs, community clean-up programs, home building programs, hospitals, crisis centers, and many more. The work that volunteers carry out in these settings is intrinsically rewarding as a result of the deep sense of satisfaction associated with

Assignment

Contact local community organizations and ask about their needs for volunteers, and ask your employees if there are organizations in which they would like to help. Put together a list of these organizations and encourage your employees to volunteer at least a few hours per quarter. You can have a special reward for the employees who put in the most volunteer hours during the year.

helping those who need a hand. At the same time, this work is extrinsically rewarding because these volunteers are often singled out for recognition not only when their projects come to an end, but at several points along the way.

Epilogue

When you encourage your employees to do volunteer work, you are opening the door for them to ascend to totally new levels of achievement, responsibility, and recognition.

85

Win That Vacation

A consistently popular reward that can give your employees a lift in every sense of the word is a paid vacation. Employees whose performance exceeds a predetermined standard or whose production leads all others are rewarded with a special trip. This reward can be provided to an individual or a team, and it works best when the performance criteria are clear and measurable, such as for employees who are in sales, collections, and production.

Assignment

If you have employees whose performance and productivity can be measured quantitatively, try rewarding the best with a paid vacation. Spell out the standards and rules, and then call your travel agent. He or she can provide you with information on transportation, accommodations, costs, and everything else you need to launch this program.

The vacations can range from an all-expenses-paid weekend at a resort or on a mini-cruise, all the way to a week or more on a fancy cruise, an exotic island, or even a safari. Employees who win should be provided with two of whatever is being offered so they can take their significant others on this journey. After all, the significant others probably spent a significant amount of time away from their winners, and this is a rewarding way to make up for that.

Epilogue

When employees go a long way to perform well, a great reward is to send them a long way as well.

86
The Field Trip

Assignment

Look at your company's significant others and pick one for your employees to visit. Contact the key player at this entity and discuss the feasibility of this type of visit. Pick a day and time that will work best for everyone, and then book it.

Just as your employees have significant others in their lives, companies have significant others, too. Some of these significant others can include major customers, suppliers, and providers of professional services, along with your home office if you are in a satellite office. An excellent way to recognize your employees for outstanding performance is to arrange a time for them to visit some of these significant others.

You can select some or all of your employees for this odyssey, depending on performance and logistics. The visit should include introductions to the key players, a tour of the facility, and a brief presentation plus time for questions and answers.

When employees are given the opportunity to visit with some of the key external forces that keep the company moving, their sense of personal value to the business increases, along with their understanding of the business itself, and this is rewarding on many levels.

Epilogue

When employees are selected to visit some of the company's important leaders, customers, vendors, or service providers, the employees feel important, too.

87

Side-by-Side With Topsiders

As new committees are formed, you can provide your best employees with high-level recognition by placing them on committees that include senior-level employees, even the president. Your employees will feel honored when selected for this type of committee, and any further accolades that come from the members or as a result of the committee's work is simply icing on this cake of recognition. With a positive experience on this committee, employees are often more likely to volunteer for other committees, and this is rewarding for the company as well as the employees themselves.

Assignment

Keep an eye out as committees are being formed, and when you learn of one that includes one or more topsiders, suggest that one or two of your best employees be included. Once they are on this committee, be sure to give them support and flexibility to attend these meetings and complete assignments that may emanate from them.

As part of their membership on this type of committee, your employees will also get to know some of the company leaders on a more individual basis. This provides them with an enhanced opportunity to learn, grow, and showcase themselves, all of which can lead to very significant rewards today and in the future.

Epilogue

One of the best ways to recognize top employees is to place them on committees that include leaders from the top of the company.

88

In Association With

Several of your employees may belong to various groups, organizations, or associations composed of individuals in their field, specialty, or profession. One of the best ways to recognize your employees' expertise is to actively encourage and support their membership in these organizations.

The best way to do this is to pay their membership dues and cover expenses for them to attend some of their association's or group's meetings, conferences, or conventions. Some of their organizations

Assignment

Let your employees know you are interested in supporting their attendance at meetings, conferences, and conventions within their specialties. Encourage them to inform you of events they would like to attend, and keep an eye out for these kinds of events on your own. If you find any that would be particularly beneficial for your employees, you should let them know and offer to pay.

may also hold special training sessions or seminars during the year, and if they make sense in terms of topics and costs, you should cover your employees to attend these as well.

Epilogue

When you send employees to conferences, conventions, and training sessions, they typically return with information, innovation, and invigoration.

89

Happy Birthday

When your employees' birthdays arrive, something should arrive from you. Even if employees prefer that you do not remember how old they are, they appreciate being remembered on this day.

Birthdays are celebrated quite differently in different companies. In some, there are elaborate parties, while in others, there may be a cupcake or less. No matter how these events are staged in your company, the most important step is to personalize the milestone with individual recognition.

The idea behind personalizing your employees' birthdays is to let them know that you are thinking about them, appreciating their work, and wishing them the best for the coming year. On a more subtle level, these actions help reinforce the family atmosphere that is rewarding and comforting for so many employees.

Assignment

Put a message into your office calendar system to remind you of your employees' birthdays. When the day arrives, regardless of any celebratory activities, be sure to provide your employee with individual birthday greetings, whether in person, by phone, by e-mail, or by card.

Epilogue

Birthday greetings from you can warm your employees' hearts, whether there are candles involved or not.

90

Cash in Hand

Whether your company pays on a weekly, biweekly, or monthly basis, you have a great opportunity to provide your employees with recognition whenever payday arrives. It is easy to let an administrative person walk around and hand checks to employees who do not use direct deposit, while handing copies of checks to those who do. Although your employees obviously appreciate receiving a paycheck, the checks tend to take on the quality of background noise when distributed this way.

Because an employee's paycheck is a form of recognition, you should personally hand the check or copy to each employee, and use the opportunity to chat briefly and voice some words of thanks and appreciation. This approach really helps your employees sense that their paychecks are a reward for excellent performance.

This approach guarantees to add at least one more individual reward and recognition session every month.

Assignment

Starting with the next payday, have all of the checks or copies delivered to you. Before you give them out, take a quick look at your employees' recent performance with an eye for key accomplishments or milestones to mention when you hand them their checks. When you meet briefly with each of them, offer some words of thanks and praise, and then hand them the checks.

Epilogue
When you distribute recognition along with the paychecks, your employees feel doubly rewarded.

114

91

In Focus

Your employees are a great resource, and they can play a very helpful role when it comes to introducing change in your company, whether such changes deal with facilities, operations, products, planning, or just about anything else.

With employee input, decisions tend to be higher quality. In addition, if the decision involves changes that affect the employees, there tends to be less resistance. It is also quite motivational for employees to participate in this process and see the actual results of their ideas and comments. And, importantly, employees sense a great deal of recognition when management includes them in these types of groups.

Assignment

The next time there is a key decision to be made, try establishing a focus group of employees to solicit their ideas and suggestions. You should make this group as diverse as possible, and be sure to provide them with thanks and recognition for their participation, along with feedback on the decisions that are ultimately made.

When employees are part of an internal focus group, the message is that they are smart, creative, and insightful. The employees sense even greater rewards when their inputs are actually incorporated into the changes that are made as a result of the group's efforts.

Epilogue

In addition to helping you make better decisions, focus groups also help you focus additional recognition on your employees.

92

Just for You

A compelling way to recognize behaviors that are particularly important in your company is to develop a unique company-specific award. By definition, this award is bestowed upon relatively few individuals, and that fact increases its value and significance for all who receive it.

Unique awards can be designed around sales, leadership, productivity, safety, attendance, suggestions, voluntarism, or any other positive behaviors that help your company fulfill its mission.

For example, if your company places a good deal of emphasis on excellent leadership, you could give out a generic leadership award, or you could do something more unique. A sample of such an award could be called "The GOLD Standard," and it would be bestowed on a leader who Gives Outstanding Leadership and Direction. This award could include a gold coin and gold embossed certificate. These types of awards are fun to create, and they are obviously fun to receive.

Assignment

Look at the key behaviors you wish to reward in your company, and single out one for a unique recognition program. Predetermine the way that you will measure success, come up with a catchy title, and be sure to include a tangible reward that fits into the theme of the program you develop.

Epilogue

Unique recognition programs have special significance in your company, and they make the recipients feel unique, special, and significant at the same time.

93

Discounts Count

Discount coupons are excellent rewards that are easy to give to your employees as spot bonuses or as part of larger events or programs. Employees at any level enjoy saving money, and discount coupons allow them to do so in many arenas that they frequent in their daily lives. With a little hunting, you can find discount coupons for restaurants, groceries, rental cars, gasoline, classes, hotels, airport parking, movies, and much more. In addition, you will be surprised to find that many restaurants and other businesses in your area are willing to offer a discount to your employees if you simply ask for one.

Assignment

Enter the phrase "discount coupons" in a search engine, and you will find a huge selection. Also, take a walk to some of the nearby businesses in your area and discuss discounts for your employees. There is a better than 10 percent chance that you can get a better than 10 percent discount from some of them.

While some companies have discount coupons that are good for one-time-use only, other companies provide small plastic cards that you can attach to your key chain and use over and over. No matter how many times an employee gets the discount, he or she again senses some of the recognition and appreciation that these discounts symbolize.

Epilogue

Discount coupons should not be discounted as important components of a recognition program.

94

Hail With the Chief

Assignment

Meet with the president of your company to discuss this program and the specific criteria on which membership should be based. Because this program is tailored to your company and the president, the two of you should also spell out the specifics of such matters as an induction ceremony, future gatherings, and tangible rewards for new honorees.

Recognition programs that link your employees with the company president are an excellent way to reward your best performers. These programs go by many names, such as the President's Circle, President's Club, President's Team, President's Forum, and President's Roundtable.

Membership should be premised on the behaviors and outcomes that are most valued by your company and by the president him- or herself. This type of recognition is often provided to a company's best salespeople, but it can just as easily be based on success in any number of other areas such as tenure, safety, employee development, voluntarism, or a combination of any of these areas.

Individuals who are selected for this honor should be given a tangible reward that is only provided for this membership. This should always include a special certificate, along with a special coat, pin, or artifact.

Epilogue

Rewarding your employees with membership in a select group chaired by the president is one of the top ways to provide topside recognition.

95

Looking Down the Road

Regardless of job level and title, many employees are interested in receiving advice on their careers. An excellent way to meet this need, recognize and reward your employees, and demonstrate your interest in their long-term growth and success is to arrange for them to receive some professional career counseling.

Your willingness to invest money in career planning and development leads the selected employees to sense that they are high performers and have high potential. This type of recognition is uplifting to them personally and can uplift their performance as well.

In addition, a career counseling program demonstrates management's interest in each employee as an individual. It is highly rewarding for employees to have clearer self-insights, a better sense of direction and goals, and specific strategies to meet them, and these too are rewarding outcomes emanating from professional career planning.

Assignment

There are excellent counselors, coaches, and organizational psychologists who can put together a tailor-made career planning program for your employees. You can find them through their professional associations, on the Internet, as well as through your network. You should interview a few of them, review their programs and costs, select one, and work with him or her to determine the best way to start with your team.

Epilogue

When you arrange for employees to receive individualized career planning, you are also arranging for them to receive individualized recognition.

96

Cards Talk

The personalized business cards that you provide to your employees obviously serve many purposes, especially when it comes to business development and networking. A less obvious role played by these cards is the recognition that is associated with them.

Many employers provide business cards for people in upper-level positions and those who regularly have face-to-face contact with customers, vendors, and others in the business world. The rest of the employees, especially those in mid-level and lower-level positions, are left without cards.

The problem is that most of these latter employees have occasions when they could actually use business cards, and when they have to scribble their name and phone number on a napkin or scrap of paper, they feel embarrassed and even insignificant. When these

> ### *Assignment*
>
> Identify all of your employees who do not currently have personalized business cards and make arrangements for all of them to have cards. If some of their titles look trivial, take a couple of steps back and consider some upgrading in this area, too.

employees are given personalized business cards, they sense that they are now truly part of the company team. These cards, independent of the holder's title, are perceived as symbols of status, stature, and importance. As such, they are highly rewarding.

Epilogue

If you're looking for a way to reward employees at all levels, keep one thought in mind: It's in the cards.

97

Make Things Pop With Balloons

A light and fun way to draw recognition to your employees is to give them a bundle of metallic helium-filled balloons for milestones they meet on or off the job. A bundle of balloons stands out like a searchlight in the night, especially if the employee works in a cubicle.

> ### *Assignment*
>
> Put together a list of upcoming milestones for each of your employees, and note the ones that lend themselves to this lighter form of recognition. In order to avoid a last minute crunch, use your phone directory and search engine today to find a suitable vendor that can provide metallic and personalized balloons.

Balloons are an excellent way to put some extra recognition on top of such upbeat workplace events as promotions, transfers, and welcoming new employees, as well as for such personal events as birthdays, graduations, and weddings. When other employees spot these balloons, they tend to come by to check out the occasion, and this further enhances and widens the reach of this type of recognition.

You can further personalize this recognition by having the employee's picture or just about any photo or comments placed onto the balloons. People typically associate balloons with fun events earlier in their lives, and when you bring them into the workplace, you help rekindle those feelings.

Epilogue

Balloons are a light and airy way to bring employee recognition to new heights.

98
Guru for a Day

Many employees have knowledge or expertise in areas that could interest their coworkers, but opportunities to share this type of information are rare in most organizations. Such areas of employee expertise can be job related, or they can deal with outside activities or hobbies.

It is very rewarding for employees to be given an opportunity to lead a discussion on topics in which they are truly experts. These employees appreciate managerial recognition of their expertise, and they also appreciate the recognition associated with leading a discussion group.

Recognition associated with this program goes beyond the presenter, as the attendees regard these sessions as learning opportunities, and that makes them inherently rewarding. Other employees will begin to think that they too would like to lead

Assignment

Ask your employees if they would like to lead a discussion on any topic within their area of expertise or general interest. Try to set these meetings once a month or once a quarter, and be sure to provide a good deal of publicity. If you include a light lunch as part of the deal, you are likely to generate even more interest.

one of these discussions, and this helps build and reinforce a corporate culture of learning and recognition.

Epilogue

When you create an opportunity for employee knowledge to be shared, you are also creating an opportunity for employee recognition to be shared.

99

Employee of the Month

The designation "Employee of the Month" is one of the more traditional forms of recognition, but that is not a shortcoming. Some of the older programs have staying power because they are still compelling sources of recognition.

Although the designation carries a great intrinsic reward, many companies sweeten this pie by attaching some attractive tangibles to it. For example, the "Employee of the Month" might be given a certificate, a trophy, a piece of jewelry, or preferred parking for the month. These tangibles are typically less

Assignment

Determine the criteria to be used in selecting an "Employee of the Month," and designate the kinds of tangible and intangible rewards to be attached to this award. You can give this program a newer spin by replacing the word "Employee" with a positive word or term of your own choosing, such as "Star," "Hero," or "Champion." Announce the program, put the publicity in place, and select your winner.

meaningful than the designation itself, but they are appreciated nonetheless.

Regardless of the tangible rewards, it is always important to have some kind of ceremony when this reward is given out, along with photos on the company Website and Wall of Fame.

Epilogue

The program is called "Employee of the Month," but the pride, satisfaction, and sense of accomplishment last a lifetime.

100

Employee of the Year

It is obviously important to provide recognition for your best employees, yet the question remains of what to do about the best of the best. That's where "Employee of the Year" enters the picture. The purpose of this award is to recognize one individual whose performance stands out above all others in all respects.

The presentation of this award is accompanied by more fanfare than other awards, and it is best done at a major company event that can include family members, board members,

Assignment

Meet with the senior management team to discuss the role and impact of this kind of reward. Work with this team to define the selection criteria, establish a selection committee, decide event and venue, and determine the rewards to be given to the winner.

and even community leaders. All of the "Employees of the

Month" should be recognized at this event, while the announcement of the "Employee of the Year" is the culmination.

To help this reward stand out even further, you can designate an entirely separate name for it, such as the "President's Award." While it is appropriate for the honoree to be given a framed certificate, the status and stature of this award merit something more, such as a trip or a cash bonus.

Epilogue

The designation of "Employee of the Year" is the ultimate in recognition for the ultimate in performance.

101

Proven Improvement

Assignment

As you track the performance of your employees over time, keep an eye out for those who are improving. At the end of the year, select the one employee who has made the greatest strides and present this award to him or her. The award should come with a certificate and a hearty round of applause.

In addition to rewarding your employees for excellence in performance, it is also important to step back and look at excellence from a different angle, specifically in terms of improved performance. You may have some employees who are showing real signs of improvement, and that calls for recognition.

One way to do this is to designate a special award for the employee who has made the greatest leap forward during the year. When an employee shows real signs of improvement and you want him or her to repeat this positive behavior, you should reinforce it, and that's exactly what an award for improved performance will do.

You can easily call this the "Most Improved Employee Award," or you can come up with a catchier name that helps give the award special meaning and significance in your company. For example, you could call it the "V.I.P. Award" for Vastly Improved Performance.

Epilogue

Rewards for the most improved employee help bring out the most in all *employees.*

102
Outside Input

If your employees have regular and direct contact with customers, such as in retail or health care, a great way to generate recognition for them is to have special recognition forms for your customers to complete on the spot. If a customer receives particularly excellent service from one of your employees, the customer should be able to easily complete a recognition form that will ultimately end up in your hands.

This form typically has your company logo, a spot for the employee's name, the date, and a section to describe the employee's excellent behavior. When an employee receives one of these forms, you should meet with him or her, review the accolades, express congratulations, and place the form in the employee's file.

> ### *Assignment*
>
> Put together the basics of this on-the-spot recognition program, and be sure to include the form, the rewards associated with the numbers of commendations that employees receive, and the publicity for the program as well as for the employees whom customers single out for recognition.

Employees should receive a congratulatory note from you each time they receive one of these commendations, and there should be additional rewards associated with additional commendations. These rewards can include certificates, pins, and a special patch if your employees wear uniforms.

> ### Epilogue
> *Recognition from outsiders has an amazingly positive and powerful impact on insiders.*

103

The Message of the Massage

High levels of pressure, tension, and stress, plus long and arduous hours, have left many of today's employees feeling tight, tense, and on edge. Feeling this way can interfere with their ability to concentrate and deal productively with others, both at work and at home.

In recognition of the employees' diligence and the stresses and strains they are experiencing, some employers are rewarding employees with massages. This entails retaining a professional masseuse to provide free massages to all interested employees.

Employees who opt to take part in this form of recognition and receive massages emerge feeling relaxed, refreshed, reenergized, and rewarded. They typically return to work with a calmer and

Assignment

Contact your healthcare providers to see if they can recommend any masseuses in your area, and check with your network and employees as well. Interview a few masseuses and discuss their programs, schedules, and fees. There are some masseuses who do a good deal of corporate work, and the individual you select must be able to help you structure your program.

clearer head, and are able to work more productively, and this is rewarding as well.

Epilogue
Providing employees with professional massages is deeply rewarding in every respect.

104
Meditate About This

Another rewarding way to help your employees cope with the pitch, fervor, and intensity of their work is to use

Assignment

Contact your health-care providers as well as local churches and temples for referrals to a meditation expert. Meet with a few of them and select the one with the best credentials, references, and experience, along with the seemingly most appropriate strategy for working with your employees. Breathe deeply and slowly, and launch the program.

the services of an expert in meditation. This individual can work with your employees on an individual and group basis to help them better handle the stresses and strains of work, gain a fresh perspective, and maintain their physical and mental well-being and balance.

On one level, meditation physically takes your employees away from the desk, computer, and cell phone, and gives them a little quiet time. On another level, the meditation expert can take your employees through exercises and experiences to help them better understand themselves and build individual tools to help them handle the challenges of their work. As a result of meditation, many people experience a sense of personal growth and insight, and they find that these outcomes help them feel better and work better.

Epilogue

A meditation expert rewards your employees with the gifts of self-insight, enhanced perspective, and a sense of well-being.

105

Ergonomically Speaking

An important way to recognize your employees for the long hours at their desks, on their computers, and on their cell phones, is to bring in an ergonomic expert to make sure that each employee is physically positioned for maximum comfort and minimum risk of injury. When it comes to furniture and furnishings, one size does not fit all. Poorly designed or positioned office furniture and equipment can lead to discomfort, muscle strains, accidents, and injury.

The areas that need specific attention in many offices include chairs, keyboard positioning and angle, height and angle of the monitor, positioning of the mouse and mouse pad, telephone placement, and height of the desk.

Assignment

Whether you are hearing complaints or not, bring in an outside expert to review the ergonomics of your employees' workstations or offices. Some experts will offer to lead group discussions on ergonomics, but you should insist on one-on-one assistance for each employee. If the expert indicates that it is time for some furniture upgrades, you should listen.

It is rewarding for employees to see that you recognize this fact and are taking action to deal with it. There are experts who can assist you, and you can find them through your workers' compensation carrier and some of the major office furniture manufacturers.

Epilogue
Furniture and office equipment should be as tailored as the user's apparel.

131

106

Feng Shui Today

As your employees work through long days and nights, papers and files pile up, and it can be difficult for anyone to get on top of the clutter except in the literal sense. An excellent way to recognize your employees' unflagging efforts to get organized is to give them some unique support in this area. One of the newest yet oldest techniques falls under the heading of feng shui, the ancient Chinese art of arranging space to fit the environment, one aspect of which is reducing clutter.

> ### *Assignment*
>
> Contact local universities and architectural and space planning firms for referrals to feng shui experts in your area. Meet with at least three experts in this field, and retain the strongest candidate for a trial run in your office. If you are satisfied with the results, give your employees a few articles on feng shui to remove the mystery and start the process with them.

An excellent reward is to bring in a feng shui expert to help your employees organize their work areas as well as their work. This can lead to improvements in their efficiency and productivity, an outcome that rewards your employees not only with more time, but also with the recognition that accompanies increases in performance.

Epilogue

When you bring a feng shui expert into your employees' lives, they soon realize that this is a reward that many have been seeking for years, often without knowing it.

107

In and About the Office

By focusing on your employees' offices or workstations, you will spot several ways to provide recognition. The size, location, and condition of the employees' offices or workstations all connote varying levels of recognition, and even a few tweaks in this area can be highly rewarding.

Assignment

Take a careful look at the physical working conditions for all of your employees and put together a list of possible improvements or changes that could be used as rewards over time. Set priorities and timeframes for each, and put this plan into motion as soon as possible.

If you want to provide employees with major recognition for their work, think about rewarding them with a large office, a corner office, an office with a view, or even an office that includes a separate table and chairs. On a smaller scale, you can generate recognition for your employees by taking such basic steps as upgrading the carpet, painting the walls, providing a new and ergonomically sound chair, or bringing in some other new furniture.

133

Your employees' physical surroundings emit a constant background message, and you can make these surroundings ring with recognition by making a few upgrades.

Epilogue

When you reward employees by improving their working conditions, you are also improving their mental condition.

108

Artful Management

When employees move into an office or from one office to another, they often inherit whatever art happens to be on the walls. In order to generate the full range of recognition associated with this type of move, employees should be provided with an opportunity to select the artwork for their walls. This does not necessarily mean that they can hang whatever they want, but they should at least be able to make their own selections from a booklet of approved art.

Assignment

Assemble a booklet of at least 100 reproductions that are suitable for your employees' office walls. Whenever employees are moved into a new or different office, they should be given the booklet and the freedom to select whatever they want. Check also with your current office-holders to see how they feel about the art on their walls, and have the booklet ready for them, too.

While art on the walls is not going to motivate your employees, it does have the potential to annoy, distract, and bother them. You can easily solve this problem with the art booklet. By letting your employees have more control over the look of the area in which they will spend most of their waking hours, you are providing visual recognition of their judgment, taste, and independence.

> **Epilogue**
> *When employees are given the opportunities to select artwork for their walls, their entire employment picture improves.*

109

A Little Shut-Eye

It is only natural that your hard-working employees are occasionally going to feel sleepy while at work. Although there is a strong negative connotation associated with sleeping on the job, a growing number of employers are stetting this stigma aside and looking more carefully at the notion of employee naps.

The result is a growing belief that an employee nap is not such a bad thing. When employees recharge their batteries with a brief nap, they give their productivity a real jumpstart, and this is rewarding to them as well as to the company.

Assignment

Let your employees know that if they need a 10- or 20-minute snooze, it is fine with you. For starters, they can do this at their desk. If you see positive results over time, then consider other accommodations, such as cots and even a power nap room.

135

In fact, some employers are now rewarding employees with an opportunity to take a brief nap during the day. The underlying message is that employees are mature adults who know what they need in order to operate at peak efficiency, even if it means a short snooze. Employers have also increased their comfort with naps by giving these breaks a more accept-able name: power naps.

Epilogue

By allowing employees to take power naps, you are open-ing your eyes to a form of recognition that is a real sleeper.

110

Taken for a Ride

One reward that is lit-erally a moving experience for the recipients is the use of a limousine. This is actu-ally a reward for two en-tirely separate audiences, one focused on the fun and the other focused on the function.

On the fun side, provid-ing employees with a limo ride to and from work for a week is a well-received re-ward for outstanding perfor-mance in any number of areas. For example, this can

Assignment

Review the possibility of using a limo service to provide fun and functional rewards to your employees. Call your contacts at other companies for referrals to a limousine service, and use your phone directory and the Internet for additional sources. Contact a few of these services for prices, references, and necessary licenses and insurance, and then get the wheels turning.

be a perfect reward for employees who win company contests for safety, carpooling, or general suggestions.

On the functional side, providing a limousine service for your frequently traveling employees is a clear help to them. It lessens the hassle and stress associated with air travel when departing and arriving. Your traveling employees greatly appreciate your understanding and recognition in this arena, and they do not need any articles or photos.

Epilogue

Use of a limousine can be an ideal reward for your driven employees.

111

Name Recognition

If you have a long-term employee who has distinguished himself or herself in a particular area, one of the greatest forms of recognition is to name an award in his or her honor. The award is built around this employee's consistently excellent performance in any area of importance to your company, such as sales, service, or creativity.

For example, one of your long-term employees, George Washington, has been a source of amazingly creative ideas for many years. In order to honor this accomplish, you would create the Washington Award, given annually to one employee whose innovative thinking best represents George's ideas and ideals.

George is greatly rewarded by having this award as a permanent legacy, and future recipients understand that they have received a truly special form of recognition, a one-of-a-kind, made even more so if George personally presents it to them.

Assignment

If you have a long-term employee who has been consistently excellent in a key area, establish an award in his or her name. At an appropriate ceremony, honor this individual by announcing this award and presenting a special certificate and trophy. Over the long term, monitor the performance of your employees to see if any of them merit your company's version of the Washington Award.

Epilogue

When you honor an employee by creating an award in his or her name, it is far more than an award in name only.

112

For All to See

If you want to have some fun and shock your employees with a huge gesture of recognition, rent space on a billboard that many employees pass on their way to work. The billboard can include a congratulatory message to an individual or team, along with a photo, artwork, and logo.

Assignment

By using your local telephone directory or a search engine, you can find numerous media companies that can rent billboard space just about anywhere, often on a monthly basis and at reasonable rates. If you are looking online, your keywords are "rent" and "billboard space." Check out pricing and timing, and try to select a spot on a route traveled by many of your employees.

This type of recognition is best used for very special accomplishments by an individual or group, and it is guaranteed to make an indelible imprint on the recipients as well as the rest of your team. You can magnify the message even further by taking pictures of the employees in front of their billboard and posting them on the company's Website and Wall of Fame.

This recognition can be part of another program, such as the "Employee of the Month," or it can literally be a standalone reward.

Epilogue

When you recognize your employees by placing compelling words of congratulations and appreciation on a billboard, it's a real sign of approval.

113

It's That Time of the Yearbook

When people hear the word, "yearbook," they often think back to the days of high school or college, without realizing that yearbooks can be a terrific source of recognition in today's workplace. Yearbooks are a great way to provide recognition and thanks to every employee for his or her hard work during the year.

A company yearbook is composed of hundreds of candid and posed photos of employees taken throughout the year. They show employees at their desks, clowning around, getting awards, attending meetings, relaxing on breaks, playing on company teams, and enjoying company events. Some of the shots may have already appeared online and on the Wall of Fame.

This yearbook can be a fairly simple booklet or something more elaborate. The only ground rule is that every employee should have at least one photo in

> ### *Assignment*
>
> Tell your employees about the yearbook and select a few of volunteers to put it together. Give them the parameters and the budget, and hold a contest for all of the employees to come up with a name. In addition to giving yearbooks to all employees, be sure to save a few for the lobby and company promotions.

it, and hopefully more. The yearbooks are then distributed to all employees at year-end, typically at a company party.

> **Epilogue**
> *Whenever employees see a shot of themselves in the company yearbook, they get a shot of recognition.*

114

On the Road

Go to any airport midweek and you will see armies of business travelers, the road warriors who spend much of their work life in taxis, airports, planes, and hotels. They are out there selling, buying, solving problems, building relationships, and keeping millions of businesses alive and well. It is easy to say that their pay is their reward, and to a certain extent this is true, but heavy-duty travelers need recognition, too.

While pins and plaques are appreciated, these individuals particularly enjoy rewards that can help them on the road. Some of the rewards that fit this bill include state-of-the-art luggage, briefcases, tote bags, currency converters, eyeshades, garment bags,

Assignment

Review the performance of your employees who spend a great deal of time on the road, and look at the formal and informal recognition they have been given in the past year. If this recognition has been thin, have a mini-ceremony and provide them with some of these travel-related rewards. If you can have their name or initials embossed on any of these items, so much the better.

luggage tags, toiletry cases, travel pillows, travel locks, and travel clocks. These employees go a long way to reach their goals, and this type of recognition literally and figuratively goes a long way.

Epilogue

Rewarding employees with items that make travel easier is an easy way to recognize your frequent flyers as well as your infrequent flyers.

115

In Cool Companies

One of the hallmarks of many of today's dynamic and successful companies, often the companies that are found on listings of the best employers, is that they are referred to as "cool companies." A cool company typically has a flat organizational structure, open communications, an open work environment, programs that reinforce work-life balance, employee participation in decision-making, and employee-friendly benefits such as support for day care and physical fitness.

Assignment

Develop a list of the kinds of cool items that you would like to give your employees, and then do some online and local checking for availability and pricing. In order to make these gifts even more special, be sure to include the company logo where feasible.

As you reward your employees, there are some fun rewards that keep the "cool" theme in mind. These are little tangible rewards that you can give out as spot bonuses, interim rewards for attendance or safety, or company-wide rewards just to say thanks to the team for their hard work.

With the "cool" theme in mind, these rewards include insulated mugs to keep drinks cool, freezer bags, fans that spray a cool mist, and coupons at the local ice cream or smoothie shop.

Epilogue

You will not get a cold reception when you reward your employees with gifts that are literally and figuratively cool.

116

Technically Speaking

Whether as prizes in contests, incentives for reaching objectives, or simply as tangible recognition to show appreciation and thanks, rewards that help make your employees' work lives and personal lives a little easier are always well received. Many of the rewards that best meet this dual goal can be found in the electronics aisles, whether you are online or on foot.

Some of these rewards include cell phones, digital cameras, laptops, iPods, hi-def televisions, home theatre systems, camcorders, photo printers, DVD players, GPS navigation receivers, and all-in-one wireless devices. These are the kinds of rewards that employees will use every day, and each time they hit the power button, they sense some of the recognition that led to this reward.

When employees are rewarded with these state-of-the-art rewards, items that they hardly knew about yesterday are indispensable today. There are not many rewards that can offer that kind of impact.

Assignment

Do some browsing at the major electronics outlets in your area. Chat with the salespeople about pros and cons of products that might be right for your star employees, and take a look at some of reviews on these items as well. As you put together your menu of rewards for your various recognition programs, be sure to include some of these items.

Epilogue

By rewarding employees with state-of-the-art electronic equipment, you are also providing them with state-of-the-art recognition.

117

It's About Time

Because many of your most productive and effective employees spend great amounts of time on their work, it is only fitting to link the notion of time to the rewards you give them. One of the best ways to make this connection is to reward these employees with a watch or a clock.

Assignment

Visit your local jewelry stores, department stores, electronic outlets, and sports stores to get a better idea of the offerings and prices, and make a similar search online by entering "watch," "clock," and "employee recognition" into one of the major search engines. You can further personalize these awards by inscribing the employee's name and a few congratulatory words.

If you decide on a watch, it is not the generic gold watch that is synonymous with a recipient's imminent trip to pasture. Rather, each watch symbolizes successful times ahead and should fit the employee who receives it, not only in terms of sizing but also in terms of style. A sports watch might work for one employee, while something more traditional might be in order for another.

The same type of thinking applies to a clock, because it should literally and figuratively fit in the employee's office or workstation, while at the same time leaving no doubt that it is an award.

Epilogue

Rewarding your employees with a watch or a clock provides them with timely recognition every time they look at it.

118

For Sparkling Performance

Rewarding your employees with jewelry is a shining example of recognition that can last a long time. However, many managers set jewelry aside because they think such rewards are appropriate only for females. The reality is that you can find a tremendous array of highly desirable jewelry for men and women in all styles, arrangements, and price ranges.

Some of the best rewards for your employees' outstanding dedication and performance start with bracelets, rings, and necklaces, and can easily include key chains, earrings, pendants, and more.

Assignment

Although you can easily wander into a jewelry store or onto an online site and find some attractive pieces of jewelry, this is no arena for amateurs. If this is unfamiliar territory to you, you should work with a knowledgeable associate who understands your employees' tastes and style. Be sure to have a budget, and stick to it.

The only caveat is that a piece of jewelry has to match the employee's taste, or it will be consigned to a jewelry box.

When an employee is given a fitting piece of jewelry to commemorate a milestone, landmark, or success, he or she wears it often, in part because of its inherent appeal, and in part because of the constant message of recognition that reflects from it.

Epilogue

Jewelry is a perfect reward for an employee who is a real gem.

119

Treats and Eats

There are times when your employees have been performing so well that they deserve a treat, and one of the most palatable rewards is something special to eat. In this regard, lunches and mid-afternoon snacks are popular items on the recognition menu.

Assignment

Check with your employees and make a list of their favorite restaurants, foods, and desserts. Contact some of the chains, restaurants, shops, and caterers that serve the most popular items, and then book one per quarter to come to your workplace.

Many of your employees' favorite restaurants provide catering, whether it's hamburgers, ethnic foods, or deli platters. You have the option of making the event as structured or casual as you would like. You can even find restaurants that will bring their catering vans to your offices, prepare several of their specialties, and then serve them to your employees right off the grill.

On the snack front, you can sweeten your employees' day by having a local ice cream shop or caterer serve some creative desserts and other delectable dishes. Many of these services will come right to your office and handle the entire event. While these food feasts are personalized in part by selecting foods the employees enjoy, you should go further by including low-carb and sugar-free choices.

Epilogue

If you reward your employees with special lunches and snacks, they eat it up.

120

One-on-One With a Pro

With a quick glance at your employees, you are likely to find that they have individual interests in such pursuits as painting, softball, golf, tennis, knitting, carpentry, fishing, and more. Each of these areas opens a door for individualized recognition.

If you would like to give your prized employees a reward they will remember, enjoy, and use for years to come, give them an hour of private time with an expert from their area of interest. For example, reward your golfing employee with a lesson from a pro. When this employee goes through the lesson, complete with videotaped guidance, he or she is going to be bursting with positive emotions, and that is the exact impact you want in a recognition program.

Assignment

If you have an outstanding employee who deserves an outstanding reward, try to learn more about his or her outside interests. Do a search for a real expert who offers lessons, and then break the good news to your employee and to the rest of the team.

Your employees' outside interests are reflections of some of their key motivations. When you provide a reward that helps fulfill these motivations, the broader message is that you are truly interested in your employees' satisfaction, happiness, and growth.

Epilogue
Rewards that help employees succeed in their non-work activities also help them succeed their work activities.

121

Your Grab Bag

It is particularly effective to time your rewards so that they are as close as possible to an employee's positive behaviors, and you can do this in an upbeat and entertaining way by having a grab bag of rewards in your office. When you catch an employee doing a great job, invite him or her into your office, pull out the bag, and let the employee pick a reward.

> ### *Assignment*
>
> Get a unique bag and fill it with coupons, tickets, gift certificates, and vouchers for some very special prizes. Let your employees know about the bag and the way the program works. When your first employee makes the first grab, make sure everyone knows.

The bag should contain all sorts of terrific items such as discount coupons, gift certificates, and movie tickets. It should also have a few coupons for some higher ticket items, such as a digital camera or a watch. When an employee earns a trip to the bag, you can invite other employees to attend the mini-ceremony if you wish. Either way, be sure to add some words of recognition, praise, and appreciation for a job well done.

Epilogue

The possibility of a rewarding trip to your grab bag is sure to grab your employees' attention.

122

Take Training Personally

In addition to the traditional organizational trainers that teach employees about leadership or motivation, there are other trainers who can teach your employees about their minds and bodies. Although these trainers do not focus directly on workplace topics, their areas of expertise contribute to the employees' physical and mental health, and that's highly rewarding for any workplace or worker.

> ### *Assignment*
>
> Contact some of the fitness centers in your area and generate a list of trainers that fall into this holistic category. Contact each of them and bring in the most promising for additional interviews and screening. Pick the best ones to start the program, and make sure that you enroll in it.

Some of the trainers who can play a key role in this type of recognition program include fitness experts, nutritionists, yoga instructors, and Pilates instructors. These trainers can meet with your employees on an individual and group basis, and build their strength, stamina, flexibility, confidence, self-image, stress management skills, general health, and even their resistance to disease.

If you stretch beyond conventional training programs and approach your employees with a more holistic approach, you will be rewarding your employees on numerous levels, hence widening and deepening the impact of your recognition program.

> **Epilogue**
> *Rewarding employees with programs that take a holistic approach is good for the whole company.*

123

It's a Picnic

If you are seeking a classical favorite recognition event, look no further than a good old company picnic, complete with burgers, ribs, potato chips, watermelons, games, contests, and prizes. Company picnics typically include all of the employees, their families, and sundry significant others. These events are often held at a park on one of the days of a long weekend.

Picnics are an upbeat way to say thanks to the employees and provide all of the attendees with a relaxing, entertaining, and fun-filled afternoon.

Picnics also create a perfect opportunity for

Assignment

Start looking for the venue for a company picnic today, because the best sites get booked early. Assemble a team of employees to help coordinate the event, and give them a clear idea of your expectations and budget. Picnics are a great time to give out awards, but whether you do so or not, be sure to offer thanks and recognition to your picnic planners.

managers to visit with employees and their families and provide public thanks and recognition. Importantly, if there are games and contests, management should participate. When managers sit in an isolated cluster at these picnics, much of the recognition goes to waste.

Epilogue

The best company picnics serve heaping portions of salads, burgers, fries, and recognition.

124
Retreat and Recharge

You can provide your employees with multiple recognition opportunities when you take them on a retreat. Typically held at a conference center or resort, and lasting anywhere from a half day to a week, retreats set the stage for you and your employees to engage in a wide range of activities to build skills, enhance teamwork, brainstorm, and play.

Employees instantly feel recognized when invited to go on a company retreat. Furthermore, once the employees are at the retreat, many of the activities, exercises, simulations, and discussion sessions place them in situations where they receive instantaneous positive feedback and recognition from their peers as well as from the managers in attendance.

> **Assignment**
>
> The first step is to find out if a retreat is right for you and your team, and then which type of retreat best fits your needs. To get your answers, contact some of the corporate retreat companies that you can easily locate in your phone directory and online. The best companies will work with you every step of the way, starting today.

Retreats also offer your employees an opportunity to gain self-insight, participate in entirely new learning activities such as ropes classes, and build better relationships with all who attend.

Epilogue

If you want to provide your employees with numerous opportunities for recognition, self-insight, and growth, do not retreat from retreats.

125

Time-Released Recognition

Several forms of recognition continue to provide rewards well into the future, but in many cases the rewards are more psychological than tangible. However, there is a great way to provide recognition that includes long-term tangible and psychological rewards.

If you have employees who have demonstrated outstanding work and goal attainment, and you want to reward them for months or even years into the future, there is a very easy step: give them a membership in a "club" that sends them special foods or beverages every month for a year or more.

In order to personalize this reward, you should pick a food or beverage that matches the tastes of your employees, and with the vast array of offerings available from these clubs, you should have no difficulty doing so. There are clubs that will send your employees a monthly gift of just about anything you can imagine, including wine, meat, cheese, salsa, fruit, vegetables, plants, coffee, tea, nuts, and much more.

Assignment

Put together a list of your employees and their favorite foods and beverages. For those whose performance merits a gift every month, use a phone directory or search engine to find companies that offer the perfect item for each selected employee.

Epilogue

Rewarding your employees with a delectable monthly gift leaves a good taste in their mouths for a long time.

126

Stress Relief

Most employees today understand the health risks associated with high levels of stress, and yet such stress is a common byproduct of hard work and long hours. While one of the byproducts of many of today's best recognition programs is a reduction in stress, such as the outcomes associated with massages and yoga, there are also some specific rewards you can give your employees to help them deal with job stress.

These rewards span across a broad continuum that includes showing a comedy movie during an extended lunch, taking advantage of the relaxing impact of the sound of water by providing employees with desktop white-noise generators or mini-fountains, and even giving employees tropical fish in their offices or workstations.

Assignment

Always be on the alert for signs of stress, such as increased illness, accidents, or irritability. If you see them, sit down with your employees and listen carefully. They can often identify the sources of stress, and you should be ready to apply any available tools to deal with them.

It is not as if these rewards are cure-alls for stress, but they can possibly provide some relief. And, on a psychological level, they send a message of care and concern to the employees, and this message can be a stress reducer in and of itself.

Epilogue

As you select and implement various recognition programs, it is important to stress the importance of stress reduction.

127

Strike a Pose

For attention-grabbing recognition that is long on fun, bring in a caricature artist to sketch your employees. You can make this a reward for a team that met an important objective by having the artist draw a picture of the entire team or individual pictures of each member. Or you need not attach the caricatures to any specific goal, but simply make them an upbeat gift for all of your employees.

Having a caricature drawn is about as personalized as recognition can get. In fact, caricaturists typically highlight the prominent characteristics and traits of their subjects and often generate highly individualized pictures. The process of having a caricature drawn is a bonding experience if several of your employees are watching and offering hints and suggestions. By placing the finished portraits on the wall in a break room or in the hallways, you can have a clearly positive impact on the atmosphere.

Epilogue
There is an art to recognizing employees, especially when you can provide employees with art that they recognize.

128

Deep-Rooted Forms of Recognition

Many employees enjoy recognition that not only highlights their accomplishments, but also has some significance beyond the workplace itself. Growing numbers of employees are becoming increasingly passionate about the environment, and you can recognize these employees and their concern for the planet by rewarding them with a tree or trees planted in their names.

This reward is particularly appropriate for employees whose performance also contains an element of social responsibility. For example, for the employee who has done the most volunteer work in the community or has been honored by another civic organization for his or her support, your donation of a tree in his or her name is a very fitting piece of additional recognition.

Assignment

As you review your employees' performance, try to find successes in the workplace and beyond. In such cases, consider honoring an employee with a tree in his or her name. You can find many organizations interested in these donations by entering "trees," "donation," and "honor" in your favorite search engine.

There are numerous schools, clubs, cities, and parks that have programs in place to receive these donations, and the idea of having a tree planted in an employee's name is a visual, long-term, and singular reward that recognizes the recipient on many levels.

Epilogue

One of the best ways to move beyond traditional recognition programs and branch into new areas is to plant a tree in your employee's name.

129

Please Pass the Recognition

As employees look for faster and cheaper ways to get to and from work, there are some excellent rewards that are sure to move them. These rewards include transit passes for buses, commuter trains, and subways, as well as speed passes for toll roads and bridges.

On the surface, these rewards save time and money, but on a deeper level, they can help reduce frustration, tension, and stress. Such rewards also help your employees get a quicker jumpstart on their work, rather than spending half an hour to decompress after a harrowing commute. By easing the transition into the workplace each day, you are helping your employees reach the rewards inherent in their work more quickly and easily.

Assignment

Contact your local transit agencies to purchase passes and vouchers appropriate for your geographical area. Be sure to tailor these transportation-related rewards to the needs of your employees, such as by providing passes for the bridge to employees who actually use the bridge.

It is important to provide rewards that employees truly appreciate and use, and anything that eases their commute is high on that list. These types of rewards work particularly well as spot bonuses, as well as for employees who carpool or use public transportation.

Epilogue

When you make it easier for your employees to get to and from work, you also make it easier for them to work.

130

Amusing Outings

When it's time to recognize your employees for their tireless dedication, there are outstanding family-friendly programs that step outside the box and outside the workplace. While these programs typically last an entire day, their objective is short and sweet: fun for the entire family.

Some of the best examples of these programs include company-sponsored trips to a zoo, aquarium, amusement park, or museum, especially a children's

Assignment

Look at the weekend sections of your local papers and you will find numerous events, activities, and venues that can be very rewarding for your employees and their families. Pick one that fits best, and start the planning process. Announce the program early, but hold back some of the specifics in order to build excitement.

museum. The company handles all of the logistics, including transportation, meals, special tours, passes that bypass long lines, and even entertainment. As part of the fun, you can give out T-shirts or hats that honor your employees' great work.

These types of events reward your team with laughter, thrills, smiles, and warm shared memories, all of which are priceless.

Epilogue

When you implement family-friendly recognition programs, you will find that families become friendlier, and that is very important for you and your hard-working employees.

131
How Random

Assignment

Make a list of your steadiest and most productive employees and match this list with the recognition and rewards that they have received from you over the past six months. If you find any who have not been adequately recognized, start the search for one of these random rewards.

There are times when you have an employee who has been consistently performing well, and you would like to reward him or her. This reward is not attached to the attainment of a specific goal, but rather is a reward for this employee's excellent long-term performance.

This is the perfect time to use a more random approach in selecting a reward and pick something different that you think your employee will appreciate. For example, this might be a piece of art or furniture for the employee's home, a unique collector's item, or perhaps an antique.

The purpose of this recognition is to thank your employee and demonstrate that you are truly satisfied and pleased with all aspects of his or her performance. This type of general recognition is a pleasant surprise for your employee, and it demonstrates that your interest extends beyond attainment of one measurable goal.

Epilogue

You can provide your consistently strong employees with a reward that is random, because the recognition associated with it is anything but random.

132

A Basket of Recognition

Recognition implies a good deal of attention for a deserving employee, and one reward that both gives and grabs attention is a basket of goodies. These baskets are colorful displays, typically filled with delectable treats. When a basket appears on an employee's desk, anyone within eyeshot knows that some serious recognition is happening.

You can make this a personalized reward by steering away from off-the-shelf baskets. If you reward your employee with a basket of foods that he or she does not like, the ingredients are going to end up in a different kind of basket, and so is the recognition that goes with it.

Assignment

Make a list of your employees and the kinds of foods that you would place in a basket for them. When an employee merits this reward, pull out the list, head for your favorite supermarket, and build the basket. Don't forget to include a card that thanks the employee for doing such a great job.

The basket should be brimming with items your employee is sure to enjoy. If he or she is a wine aficionado or a cheese lover, or both, then fill the basket with that in mind. In addition to food, don't forget that you can add special rewards to the basket, such as coupons or cash.

Epilogue

A basket filled with an employee's favorite items gives a taste of recognition whenever one of those items is opened and enjoyed.

133
Significant Assignments

Some of the greatest rewards are generated by work itself, especially if the work is significant, challenging, and varied. When employees complete difficult high-level projects, they receive rewards from two different sources, both of which play premier roles in the recognition process.

One major source of recognition is actually from the employee him- or herself. When employees stretch themselves to undertake and complete assignments that seemed beyond their reach, they experience high levels of self-satisfaction, self-worth, and achievement, all of which are major psychological rewards with long-lasting positive effects.

The second key source of rewards is the employee's manager. When an employee completes a Herculean project, the best managers seize this outcome and provide appropriate recognition and rewards.

> **Assignment**
>
> Ask your employees for a brief summary of the work they do each day for a week, along with the degree of challenge that such work offers. If you find that too much time is spent on routine tasks, try to remove such tasks and reassign them to the appropriate individuals.

Epilogue

Projects that are meaningful and significant lead to recognition that is meaningful and significant.

134

For the New Hires

It takes time for new hires to adjust to the company's culture and truly feel like part of the team. An excellent way to accelerate this process and simultaneously provide recognition is to institute a quarterly lunch that includes all employees hired during the quarter plus the president or a key topsider. The new hires sense a good deal of recognition simply by being invited to a lunch like this, and the recognition is compounded when they actually interact with a company leader during the session.

These lunches work best when the leader makes a short presentation that covers a little history and a lot of the future. The presentation should be followed by a question-and-answer discussion and an opportunity for the employees to provide suggestions. The leader should be generous with positive feedback during these sessions and afterward, as this is one of the most compelling forms of recognition.

Epilogue

A lunch that includes all new hires and the company president or another topside leader validates the employees' sense of self-worth and value, while also validating management's commitment to be open, communicative, and responsive.

135

A Good Sign

Recognition implies sending positive messages to employees for excellent work, and one proven way to send any message is with an interior sign. These signs identify your employees by name, followed by personalized laudatory comments about their accomplishments or milestones.

One option is the old-fashioned sign with slots where you insert individual letters to spell out an employee's name and your words of praise. However, these signs are becoming woefully outdated.

A better option is a light-emitting diode (LED) sign. These are TV monitors or LED displays where your messages of recognition can appear statically or they can scroll across the sign, much like the stock tickertape. You can easily create personalized messages with a PC or wireless remote, and there are many options in terms of fonts, sizes, and colors. These attention-grabbing signs are most effective when placed in highly trafficked areas.

Assignment

You can find LED signs through your phone book or favorite search engine. After chatting with a few representatives, write out the pros and cons of introducing this signage in your company. As you do so, remember that these signs are valuable not only for recognizing employees, but also for imparting additional information to them.

Epilogue

With today's high-tech signage options, you can create highly visible recognition messages that are literally quite moving.

136

It's Your Day

For an individual employee or group that has performed re-remarkably well and truly helped the entire company, a fitting reward is to establish one day as their special day. This day would bear their name or names, and there would be events throughout the day to honor them.

This day could include a major ceremony where these individuals are recognized, widespread congratulatory posters and decorations, major online recognition, a lunch in their honor, and a special announcement from the president of the company.

Assignment

Review the performance of your employees as individuals and teams, looking for any whose contributions have clearly made a major difference in the success of your company. Let the topside leadership know that such special performance deserves a special day of recognition.

These employees could also receive appropriate certificates and individualized gifts, and then be allowed to leave early. Perhaps their early departure would be the prelude to a company-paid weekend at a resort.

When employees receive this type of honor, they understand that it is not only coming from their manager, but from the company at large. This makes the significance of this form of recognition that much larger for them.

Epilogue

Giving stellar employees their own special day is a great way to recognize the many special days they have given to the company.

167

137

The Rewards of Retirement Plans

Having a retirement plan is an important way to reward your employees today and many years from today. With employees at all job levels thinking more about their financial future, a retirement plan demonstrates that you share this concern with them. The more that you are in sync with your employees, the more rewarding it is for them to work for you and with you.

There are several kinds of retirement plans, and the best plan depends on numerous factors specific to your organization. With some expert advice, you can determine whether you should opt for a profit-

> **Assignment**
>
> If you do not have a profit-sharing plan, contact at least five of the major financial houses that provide these services and meet with representatives from each. Put together a spreadsheet that compares and contrasts their plans in terms of costs and services, and then meet with senior management with your recommendations.

sharing plan, a deferred profit-sharing plan, a 401(k) plan, or any of several other plans in this arena.

By selecting the best plan for you and your team, you will be helping your employees gain a higher degree of control over the financial side of their lives, and that is one of the greatest rewards you can give them and their significant others.

Epilogue
A retirement plan is rewarding to your employees every day, and it helps them retire more comfortably every night.

138

Bonus Time

A bonus program is yet another excellent way to recognize and reward superior performance, particularly over a stipulated period of time, such as one year. However, it is important for all of the players to understand the criteria that are used to determine bonuses.

One way to structure these programs is for a manager to jointly establish specific goals with the employee, and then make the bonus dependent on a combination of the employee meeting his or her goals and the company meeting its goals. When an employee earns that bonus, it should not simply show up in his or her paycheck, but rather should be presented in a one-on-one congratulatory meeting with the manager.

Assignment

If your company does not have a bonus plan, meet with management to discuss the possibility of implementing one. At the same time, if your company already has such a program, review the criteria that are used for bonus decisions, and if bonuses have become routine, meet with management to discuss ways to bring performance back into the equation.

For bonuses to have a psychologically rewarding impact, they need to be linked to performance. If they are viewed as something that employees are automatically entitled to receive, their value declines in all senses.

Epilogue

The word "bonus" comes from the Latin word for "good," and there's no question that a bonus is a good way to reward good performance.

139

Other Options

An important way to provide your employees with the possibility of substantial financial rewards is to have a stock option program. With this program, your employees are granted the right to buy a specified number of shares of company stock at a price and time determined by the company.

Although there are no guarantees that employees will ultimately reap heaps of money through this process, especially because issues such as market volatility, company performance, and vesting can all play a role, employees appreciate the possibility of being able to earn money in addition to their salary if they continue to perform well over time.

Assignment

If your company does not have a stock option program, meet with management to discuss this matter. And if it does have such a program, meet with a financial advisor to make sure you understand exactly how it works. This is important for you, your team, and the individuals you may be trying to hire.

In addition, a stock option plan helps employees feel more like partners and even owners in the company, and this is a major psychological reward. Importantly, it is a reward that can be given to all employees, as stock options need not be limited to executives.

Epilogue

When it comes to providing recognition and rewards, you have many options, the most apparent of which are stock options.

140

Your Talented Team

Your company is probably loaded with talented employees, not only in terms of their ability to handle their work, but also in terms of less obvious talents they may possess. For a fun-filled and rewarding activity, set aside a lunch for employees to demonstrate some of these hidden talents.

This is a time for your employees to showcase their skills as singers, dancers, stand-up comics, impressionists, musicians, poets, karaoke artists, and more. If they wish, they can group together and put on a skit. All employees are

Assignment

Put out the word that there is going to be a company talent contest, and entrants are invited in all conceivable categories. Select a date that is likely to be less busy, possibly a Friday toward the end of the month, purchase the prizes, and have the camera and video cameras ready for some fun visuals for the company Website.

invited to participate, and the employees will be the judges as well.

All entrants will be showered with applause and cheers, and there should be prizes for the best talent in each category. You can have fun with these prizes if you tailor them to each category, such as tickets to a comedy club for the funniest individual or skit.

Epilogue

When you create and conduct an event that showcases and rewards the employees' special talents, you are also showcasing some of your special managerial talents.

141

The Awards Banquet

Assignment

Contact some of the hotels and clubs in your area and put together a spreadsheet that includes sizes of meeting rooms, menu options, costs, and available dates. Meet with the other decision-makers in your company to review your spreadsheet and the feasibility of holding this type of banquet.

As the culmination for outstanding work throughout the year, one gratifying way to recognize your employees' accomplishments is to hold an awards banquet. This is typically an off-site event that includes all employees, their significant others, board members, and other guests who are important to the company.

The event can include music and entertainment, but the real highlight is the presentation of awards. The first group to be recognized should be those employees who have earned other company awards during the year, such as Employee of the Month. The banquet can also be the time to give out other special company honors and awards, such as for productivity, safety, and suggestions. The highlight of the event is the announcement of the Employee of the Year.

All of the employees feel honored to attend these kinds of events, and if they are singled out for recognition as an individual or as part of a team, their pride and satisfaction soar.

Epilogue

At the best awards banquets, the menu includes abundant servings of savory foods and recognition.

142

Great Saves

If you have employees whose actions have generated significant savings, it seems rather fitting for your company's screensaver to give them some special recognition. Instead of a generic screensaver that appears when your employees boot up, you can now personalize the company screensaver with a photo of the employees you want to recognize. This is not difficult to do if your company has centrally controlled computer systems.

Your employees' actions can lead to all sorts of savings, such as ways to save money, save energy, save a customer, save time, or save raw materials. With many of today's screensaver software packages, you can design a screensaver that includes a photo of these employees, a caption about whatever they saved, and even some background music.

173

> ### *Assignment*
>
> Check out the range of screensaver software packages at any of the major electronics outlets or online by entering "personalized" and "screensaver" into your favorite search engine. Discuss the feasibility of implementing one of these programs with whoever handles information technology at your company, and, if it can be done, do it.

> ### Epilogue
> *Placing an employee's photo on the company's screensaver is a form of recognition that gets a little kick every time the employee boots up.*

143

A Word of Advice

If you are interested in simultaneously providing recognition, building employee motivation, increasing satisfaction, and making better decisions, all you have to do is invite one or more employees into your office and ask for their advice, input, and suggestions on one of your projects.

Briefly explain the project and the strategies you have been using, and then tell the employees that you are interested in their perspective and insights. Give them an opening question and let the discussion go wherever the employees carry it. All you need to do is take notes and ask follow-up questions.

> ### *Assignment*
>
> Review your mix of ongoing projects and look for any that you might be able to manage more effectively with some advice from your team. If you find one, invite a few of your employees who are particularly skilled in your project's subject area to meet with you for some brainstorming. Regardless of the outcome, be sure to thank them for their help.

By including your employees in some of your important projects, you are treating them as valued resources, and this is highly rewarding to them. As you continue working on the project to its completion, be sure to give your employees feedback on the final results.

> ### Epilogue
> *When it comes to recognizing and rewarding employees, one of the best pieces of advice is to ask for their advice.*

144

While You Were Out

Many managers overlook an important recognition opportunity when employees return to work after being ill for a few days or longer. These employees are often greeted with hundreds of e-mail messages, but not one message indicating that anyone really cares. All of the messages tend to be all business. A little recognition at this point costs nothing, and yet it is quite meaningful.

A manager can make a major difference by taking a minute or two to send the returning employee an e-mail or meet with him or her to say, "Welcome back. We missed you." With these few words, the employee feels appreciated, valued, and important to the company.

When employees return to work after being sick and hear nothing from their manager, they tend to think the worst, and that certainly does not bring out their best.

Epilogue

When you welcome an employee who returns to work after being ill, your comments help him or her feel better and work better.

145
A True Open Door Policy

Having a true open door policy means that employees are welcome in your office, and you are genuinely interested in them and in what they have to say. This is rewarding to your employees because it shows that they are valued resources who deserve to be treated with trust and respect. This differs markedly from a classic open door policy in which employees are free to walk into a manager's office, but do so at their own peril.

When employees have questions about their work, concerns over their careers, conflicts with peers or superiors, or confusion over priorities, it is both comforting and rewarding for them to know they can sit down and have a professional and confidential discussion with their manager on these matters and just about any others. Even if employees rarely drop in on their managers, it is also rewarding for them to know they can always do so.

Assignment

Look honestly at your open door policy and make one list of the factors indicating that it is true open door policy, and another list of the factors indicating that it is a classical open door policy. If the latter is longer than the former, go back to the latter list and write a correction plan for every item on it.

Epilogue

An open door policy can be quite rewarding, provided that the manager who implements it has an open mind as well.

177

146

Let's Get Oriented

There is a good deal of bravado associated with hiring new employees, casting them into the corporate waters, and letting them sink or swim on their own, but the truth is that a well-structured orientation is far more rewarding to new employees. When new hires are left to fend for themselves, they tend to expend a great deal of time and energy on frustrating minor transitional activities, while their central job responsibilities are left untouched.

> **Assignment**
>
> Look at your orientation and whether it includes such key components as introductions, company overview, tours, training on the company's computers, and a review of key policies and programs. Talk to employees who were hired in the last six months and ask their opinion of the way they were oriented. If the orientation falls short of the mark, put together a team to rebuild it.

The sooner the new employees can get to the heart of their jobs, the sooner they sense the satisfaction that comes from learning, achieving, and meeting significant goals. With a slipshod orientation program, the message is that new employees are not particularly important, and anything that anyone else is doing is more important than orienting them. This approach starts these employees off on the wrong foot, a foot that is likely to head toward the exit.

> **Epilogue**
> *An orientation program is the first opportunity to show new hires the value that you place on recognition and on the new hires themselves.*

147

The Sky's the Limit

When employees soar to new heights in terms of performance, one very fitting reward, whether in conjunction with other rewards or on its own, is a hot-air balloon ride or a helicopter tour. These are exciting rewards in and of themselves, and they work particularly well as an add-on for other rewards, such as a weekend vacation that includes one of these rides.

Many of your employees have probably never experienced these adventures, which makes these rewards both unique and memorable. As years go by, employees may or may not remember much about a weekend vacation that

Assignment

If any of your employees have reached new records in productivity, sales, or other criteria that are key benchmarks for success in your company, use your local directory or preferred search engine to find companies that provide helicopter tours or hot-air balloon rides. Pick the one that best fits your recognition program, and then reward your high-flying employees with the uplifting news. When they go airborne, be sure to encourage them to take lots of pictures.

was awarded to them; however, if that vacation included one of these rides, the employees will remember it as if it happened yesterday. Most importantly, they will feel as if they were just rewarded yesterday.

Epilogue

For employees whose performance is above and beyond all others, a most memorable reward is one that carries them above and beyond all others.

148
Lateral Moves

One occasionally misunderstood method to recognize and reward employees is with a transfer from one job to another. Some managers and employees still regard such a move as a punishment or vote of no confidence, but nothing could be further from the truth.

A transfer is designed to take solid and productive employees and provide them with new and challenging responsibilities that better match their knowledge, skills, and abilities. When you transfer your employees, the real message is that you understand them as individuals, and you are rewarding them with increased opportunities to learn, grow, and advance.

Employees and jobs are dynamic entities, and both change over time. Sometimes they grow together, and sometimes they grow apart. When excellent employees start to diverge from the jobs, a transfer can be a great reward for the employee and the company.

Assignment

The best way to capitalize on the benefits associated with employee transfers is to have a job-posting system that lets current employees apply for open positions in the company if they wish. If your company has such a program, make sure that it is well publicized and functional. If it does not have one, start the process to have one in place over the next few months.

Epilogue

Although a job transfer moves employees sideways, it does not cast them aside, but simply casts them in a better role.

149

360 Degrees of Freedom

One of the best rewards you can provide to your employees is accurate feedback that they can use as a foundation for growth, development, and success. While you can singly provide them with feedback, one of today's most effective strategies is to provide them with 360-degree feedback.

With 360-degree feedback, employees receive feedback from their manager, their peers, and their subordinates if they have any. As part of this process, employees may provide self-evaluations. The findings are summarized by the manager and fed back to the employees along with an individualized development plan and follow-up over time.

Assignment

If you are currently using 360-degree feedback, review the effectiveness of your program by polling your employees and asking for suggestions. Use their feedback to make corrections and upgrades. If you are not using 360-degree feedback, do some reading about the process, discuss it with peers who already may be using it, discuss it with your employees, and then launch the program.

Employees view their participation in this program as a form of recognition, and they particularly appreciate accurate feedback that can help them become more effective in all senses of the word.

Epilogue
Three hundred and sixty degree feedback can reward your employees with a world of information to help them make the next positive step in their job, career, and life.

150

Recipe for Success

A fun way to recognize and reward the talent and uniqueness of your staff is to put together a company cookbook that contains your employee's favorite recipes for any meal of the day or for snacks. If your employees would like to include artwork, drawings, or photos with their culinary delights, so much the better.

On one level, the cookbook recognizes your employees as individuals. You have employees from diverse backgrounds and cultures, and a wonderful and tasteful way to honor and celebrate their individuality is a cookbook that includes their traditional recipes.

Assignment

Ask for a few volunteers to head up the company cookbook project. Give them the expectations, parameters, and budget. Let them know that there should be enough copies for every employee, and some extras for the lobby as well as for various visitors to the company. Once all of this is decided, turn the team loose.

At the same time, creating this cookbook can be a rewarding team-building exercise as employees work together to bring in their recipes and provide their inputs on how the book should be designed, organized, and assembled. Teambuilding is further enhanced when the employees share in the satisfaction that comes from seeing the finished product, a corporate cookbook that makes all of them feel proud.

Epilogue

A company cookbook can cook up all sorts of recognition for your employees.

183

151

The Best Rewards

If you would like a rewarding way to determine the best recognition programs for your employees, all you have to do is ask them. Employees know how they would like to be rewarded, and soliciting their input in the early stages of the process is rewarding, too.

Employers can go to great expense to provide their employees with rewards that are met with a yawn at best and a frown at worst. When this happens, the negative messages abound. Employees can believe that management really does not know or even care about them, and they are further distressed because the company is wasting money on meaningless rewards rather than simply giving the money to them.

Assignment

Meet with your employees to discuss your company's reward and recognition programs. Tell them about the kinds of programs you are considering, and ask for their suggestions. When you ultimately select and implement any recognition and reward program, try to tailor it to your employees' needs, and be sure to monitor its impact carefully.

As a result, in order to have highly successful recognition programs, it is important to keep the lines of communication with your employees wide open, as well as to track the effectiveness of the rewards and recognition that you provide.

Epilogue

Employees have some terrific ideas about recognition and rewards, and when their ideas are taken into consideration, the outcomes can be terrific, too.

INDEX

185

Index

189

About the Author

Ken Lloyd, Ph.D., is a nationally recognized consultant, author, and newspaper columnist based in Encino, California. With specialties in organizational behavior, management training and development, and communication, Dr. Lloyd has consulted in a wide range of industries including health care, apparel, financial services, electronics, Internet service provider, and entertainment. His workplace advice column can be found in newspapers across the United States.

He is the author of the widely acclaimed *Jerks at Work: How to Deal With People Problems and Problem People* (Career Press, 1999; revised edition, 2006), available in numerous languages including Chinese, Japanese, Polish, and Korean. He also authored *Be the Boss Your Employees Deserve* (Career Press, 2002), and he co-authored *Ultimate Selling Power: How to Create and Enjoy a Multimillion Dollar Sales Career* (Career Press/Penguin Books, 2002), along with the best-selling book *Unlimited Selling Power: How to Master Hypnotic Selling Skills* (Prentice Hall, 1990), now in its ninth printing and available in numerous languages. Dr. Lloyd is also the author of *The K.I.S.S. Guide to Selling* (DK Publishers, 2001), part of Dorling Kindersley's popular Keep It Simple Series. He also wrote the business film *Communication: The Name of the Game* (Roundtable Films and Video), award winner at the National Educational Film Festival and the American Film Festival.

Dr. Lloyd is a frequent television and talk-radio guest, and he has appeared on "Good Morning America," CNN, "Morning Edition" on NPR, along with several appearances on KABC, KTLA, and Fox Morning News "Ask the Expert" segments.

191

He received his B.A. from UC Berkeley, and his Ph.D. in organizational behavior from UCLA. He teaches frequently in the MBA program at the Anderson Graduate School of Management at UCLA, and he continues to lecture at various universities and speak before numerous organizations and associations. Dr. Lloyd is a member of the American Psychological Association and the Society for Industrial and Organizational Psychology.